Supplement to Inside the Microsoft Build Engine: Using MSBuild and Team Foundation Build, Second Edition

Sayed Ibrahim Hashimi
William Bartholomew

PUBLISHED BY
Microsoft Press
A Division of Microsoft Corporation
One Microsoft Way
Redmond, Washington 98052-6399

Library of Congress Control Number (PCN): 2013935725
ISBN: 978-0-7356-7816-3

Microsoft Press books are available through booksellers and distributors worldwide. If you need support related to this book, email Microsoft Press Book Support at mspinput@microsoft.com. Please tell us what you think of this book at *http://www.microsoft.com/learning/booksurvey.*

"Microsoft and the trademarks listed at *http://www.microsoft.com/about/legal/en/us/IntellectualProperty/ Trademarks/EN-US.aspx* are trademarks of the Microsoft group of companies. All other marks are property of their respective owners."

The example companies, organizations, products, domain names, email addresses, logos, people, places, and events depicted herein are fictitious. No association with any real company, organization, product, domain name, email address, logo, person, place, or event is intended or should be inferred.

This book expresses the author's views and opinions. The information contained in this book is provided without any express, statutory, or implied warranties. Neither the authors, Microsoft Corporation, nor its resellers, or distributors will be held liable for any damages caused or alleged to be caused either directly or indirectly by this book.

Acquisitions Editor: Devon Musgrave
Developmental Editor: Devon Musgrave
Project Editor: Valerie Woolley
Editorial Production: Christian Holdener, S4Carlisle Publishing Services
Technical Reviewer: Marc Young w/ CM; Technical Review services provided by Content Master, a member of CM Group, Ltd.
Copyeditor: Susan McClung
Indexer: Jean Skipp
Cover: Twist Creative • Seattle and Joel Panchot

I would like to dedicate this book to my parents Sayed A. Hashimi and Sohayla Hashimi. Without them I wouldn't be here to write this book.

—SAYED

I dedicate this book to my parents Rosanna O'Sullivan and Roy Bartholomew for their unending support and to Lauren Taylor and Jillian Bartholomew for the joy they bring each day.

—WILLIAM

Contents at a glance

Contents

What do you think of this book? We want to hear from you!

Microsoft is interested in hearing your feedback so we can continually improve our
books and learning resources for you. To participate in a brief online survey, please visit:

microsoft.com/learning/booksurvey

Chapter 2 **What's new in Team Foundation Build 2012** **29**

Foreword

Ah, the thankless life of the Build Master. If they do their job well, you'll never know they exist! If they don't, well, everyone knows it's the Build Master's fault, right?

I've been a builder in one form or another since my first foray into managing the build. Nearly 15 years ago now, I worked on an extremely large system with a team of hundreds. When it came time to build, we used Fred's machine. Yes, I learned that day that we built and shipped large systems on Fred's laptop.

This is also how I came to find that learning a new build system is similar to boiling a frog. If you throw a frog into hot water, it jumps out. But if you turn the water up slowly, the frog doesn't realize it's getting hot, so it stays in the pot and gets boiled. The team didn't realize how big the system had become and how complex the build was getting.

I realized immediately, somewhat intuitively, that we needed build box. Fast-forward some years, and now every group I work with uses Continuous Integration. Groups I work with have build farms, one with a "Siren of Shame," a flashing light to effectively shame the build-breaker. We have build artifacts as complex and elegant as actual preconfigured virtual machines that pop out the end of our build.

All this was made possible by the power of automation and the surprising flexibility of MSBuild. Sayed and William have written what amounts to the "missing manual" for MSBuild. MSBuild, and its enterprise support counterpart Team Foundation Build, are almost unapologetically powerful. However, they need to be.

Today's software systems are multilayered, multitiered, and iterate at a speed previously unheard of. All our software development practices and team building comes together at one pinch point: the build.

This essential reference to MSBuild gives us the knowledge not only into how to create an adaptable and vigorous build system, but also valuable insights into the "why" of the product. William is a senior development lead on engineering systems within the Developer division at Microsoft, while Sayed is a program manager overseeing build and pushing for the Microsoft Azure Cloud and Web Tools. I could think of no better people to help me understand a large build system than the folks building large systems themselves.

Sure, we've all started with "Build.bat" and called it our build system. Perhaps we've put together a little schedule and called it an automated build. But these simple constructs don't scale across a large team or a large product. This book is what the documentation should have been—a guide that takes us through the humble beginnings of MSBuild as a supporting and unseen player in the .NET ecosystems to complete and sophisticated team build solutions.

More importantly, Sayed and Bill dig into the corners and edge cases that we all find ourselves bumping up against. They elaborate on the deceptively deep extensibility model that underlies MSBuild and give us the tools to bring both stock and custom components together into a complete team workflow.

MSBuild continues to evolve from version 2, to 3.5, and now to version 4 and beyond. This updated supplemental edition builds (ahem) on the good work of the previous editions and includes new sections on the updates to the MSBuild core, changes in Team Build, and even updates to Web Publishing in Microsoft Visual Studio 2012.

I'm glad that this book exists and that people who care about the build like Sayed and William exist to light the way. Now, if I can just find out what I did just now that broke my build . . .

— *Scott Hanselman*
Teacher, coder, blogger, podcaster
hanselman.com

Introduction

Build has historically been kind of like a black art, in the sense that there are just a few people who know and understand it and are passionate about it. But in today's evolving environment, that is changing. Now more and more people are becoming interested in build and making it a part of their routine development activities. Today's applications are different from those that we were building 5 to 10 years ago. Along with that, the process that we use to write software is different as well. Nowadays, it is not uncommon for a project to have sophisticated build processes that include such things as code generation, code analysis, unit testing, automated deployment, and so on. To deal with these changes, developers are no longer shielded from the build process. Developers have to understand the build process so that they can employ it to meet their needs.

Back in 2005, Microsoft released MSBuild, which is the build engine used to build most Microsoft Visual Studio projects. That release was MSBuild 2.0. Since that release, Microsoft has released three major versions of MSBuild—MSBuild 3.5, MSBuild 4.0, and now MSBuild 4.5. Along with the updates included in MSBuild 4.5, there are many build-related updates in related technologies. For example, with Visual Studio 2012, you now have the ability to share projects with Visual Studio 2010. Another great example is the usage of *NuGet*. In many ways, *NuGet* has changed how we develop and build applications. In this book, we will look at the updates included in MSBuild 4.5, as well as other related technologies.

Team Foundation Build (or Team Build as it is more commonly known) is now in its fourth version. Team Build 2005 and Team Build 2008 were entirely based on MSBuild, using it for both build orchestration and the build process itself. Team Build 2010 moved build orchestration to Microsoft Windows Workflow Foundation and continues to use MSBuild for the low-level build processes. Team Build 2012 continues this architecture but now supports building in the cloud using the Team Foundation Service, an updated task-focused user interface, gated check-in improvements to improve throughput, and better support for unattended installation.

When developing automated build processes, the next step in many cases is to automate the publish process. In Visual Studio 2010, the initial support for the Web Deploy tool was added. In Visual Studio 2012, there have been a lot of updates to how web projects are published, including first-class support for publish profiles from the command line, sharing of publish profiles with team members, database publishing, and many more. In this update, we will describe these updates and show you some real-world examples as well. You'll see how the process used in Visual Studio 2012 is much more straightforward than what was provided in Visual Studio 2010.

Who should read this book

This book is an enhancement to our *Inside the Microsoft Build Engine, Using MSBuild and Team Foundation Build, Second Edition* (Microsoft Press, 2011), a book whose content is still relevant and accurate. Rather than add these three chapters to that book and release it as a third edition, we decided to offer this shorter (and cheaper) supplement. Think of the three chapters in this supplement as an addition to *Inside the Microsoft Build Engine*.

The second edition and this supplement to it were written for anyone who uses or is interested in using MSBuild or Team Build. If you're using Visual Studio to build your applications, you're already using MSBuild. *Inside the Microsoft Build Engine* and its supplement are for all developers and build masters using Microsoft technologies. If you're interested in learning more about how your applications are being built and how you can customize this process, you need these books. If you are using Team Build or thinking of using it tomorrow, these books are must-reads. They will save you countless hours.

The second edition and this supplement will help the needs of enterprise teams as well as individuals. To get the most out of these materials, you should be familiar with creating applications using Visual Studio. You are not required to be familiar with the build process, but if you are not, make sure to begin with the second edition because it starts with the basics and goes on from there. Because one of the most effective methods for learning is through examples, both the second edition and this supplement contain many examples.

Assumptions

To get the most from this supplement, you should meet the following profile:

- You're familiar with MSBuild 4.0 and Team Foundation Build 2010.

- You should be familiar with Visual Studio.

- You should have experience with the technologies you are interested in building.

- You should have a solid grasp of XML.

Who should not read this book

This supplement to *Inside the Microsoft Build Engine* covers the new and changed functionality in MSBuild 4.5 and Team Foundation Build 2012, so it's not aimed at people new to MSBuild and Team Foundation Build. If you're new to MSBuild and Team Foundation Build, we highly recommend reading *Inside the Microsoft Build Engine* first.

Organization of this book

This book is divided into three chapters, each of which focuses on a different build technology. Chapter 1, "What's new in MSBuild 4.5," covers the new and changed functionality in MSBuild 4.5, including compatibility with previous versions, out-of-process tasks, and *NuGet*. Chapter 2, "What's new in Team Foundation Build 2012," covers the new and changed Team Foundation Build functionality, including the introduction of Team Foundation Online, a new customizable task-focused user interface, improved debugging and administration, and a number of gated check-in improvements. Chapter 3," What's new in web publishing", includes details on the updated web publish experience in Visual Studio 2012. This includes updates to publish profiles, database publishing support, web.config transform updates and more.

Conventions and features in this book

This book presents information using conventions designed to make the information readable and easy to follow.

- Each exercise consists of a series of tasks, presented as numbered steps (1, 2, and so on) that list each action you must take to complete the exercise.

- Boxed elements with labels such as "Note" provide additional information or alternative methods for completing a step successfully.

- Text that you type (apart from code blocks) appears in **bold. In code blocks code in bold indicates code added since the previous example.**

System requirements

You will need the following hardware and software to complete the practice exercises in this book:

- One of Windows 7 (x86 or x64), Windows 8 (x86 or x64), Windows Server 2008 R2 (x64), or Windows Server 2012 (x64).

- Visual Studio 2012, any edition (multiple downloads may be required if using Express edition products)

- Computer that has a 1.6 GHz or faster processor

- 1 GB (32-bit) RAM (add 512 MB if running in a virtual machine)

- 10 GB of available NTFS hard disk space

- 5,400 RPM hard disk drive

- DirectX 9 capable video card running at 1,024 x 768 or higher-resolution display

- DVD-ROM drive (if installing Visual Studio from DVD)

- Internet connection to download software or chapter examples

Depending on your Windows configuration, you might require Local Administrator rights to install or configure Visual Studio 2012.

You will need the following minimum level of hardware and software to use the virtual machine used for the practical exercises in Chapter 2 of this book:

- Either Windows Server 2008 R2 with the Hyper-V role enabled, Windows Server 2012 with the Hyper-V role enabled, or Windows 8 with Hyper-V enabled

- Intel VT or AMD-V capable processor (SLAT-compatible processor required if using Windows 8)

- 6 GB of free physical RAM (8 GB or more is recommended)

- 3 GB of RAM assigned to the virtual machine (4 GB or more is recommended)

- 50 GB of available NTFS hard disk space (more is recommended if using snapshots)

Code samples

Most of the chapters in this book include exercises that let you interactively try out new material learned in the main text. All sample projects, in both their pre-exercise and post-exercise formats, can be downloaded from the following page:

http://aka.ms/MSBuild2ESupp/files

Follow the instructions to download the MSBuild2ESupp_678163_Companion Content.zip file.

> **Note** In addition to the code samples, your system should meet the System Requirements listed previously.

Installing the code samples

Follow these steps to install the code samples on your computer so that you can use them with the exercises in this book.

1. Unzip the MSBuild2ESupp_678163_CompanionContent.zip file that you downloaded from the book's website to C:\InsideMSBuild\.

2. If prompted, review the displayed end user license agreement. If you accept the terms, select the Accept option, and then click Next.

> **Note** If the license agreement doesn't appear, you can access it from the same webpage from which you downloaded the MSBuild2ESupp_678163_CompanionContent.zip file.

Using the code samples

After extracting the samples you will see a folder for each chapter. Within each subfolder you will find all the samples for that chapter.

Acknowledgments

The authors are happy to share the following acknowledgments.

Sayed Ibrahim Hashimi

Wow. This will be my fourth book and my third with Microsoft Press. I'm not sure how I ended up here, but it certainly was not on my own. Throughout each book there were key contributors who helped us create the final product. Even though this book is much smaller than my previous ones, it's still no easy task. We still have to go through the entire process and involve basically the same number of people to help us. Being an author, I receive a majority of the credit for the result, but there are plenty of others who deserve credit as well.

I'd like to start by thanking my co-author, William Bartholomew. William also works at Microsoft. William is a known Team Build expert, and it shows in his writing. I've had so many people approach me and tell me how good the Team Build chapters are. Most times, I smile and quietly accept the praise—that's part of being a co-author—thanks, William! William has helped me since the first edition of this book. I love working with him and hope that I can do so again in the future.

In the second edition, we had a wonderful technical editor, Marc Young. Thankfully, we were able to convince him to come on board for this supplement as well. I'm really glad that we were able to do so. He did a brilliant job on the second edition and a great job for this supplement, too. Marc is not shy when it comes to letting authors know that they are wrong! He goes to great lengths to verify, or disprove, author statements and code samples. I appreciate all of his efforts, and readers should as well. His feedback is also critical in shaping the content of the book.

Devon Musgrave, the man behind the scenes at Microsoft Press, deserves a lot of credit here. I remember having dinner with Devon in Bellevue one night in the summer of 2012. We discussed the idea of an update to the book. We both knew that a full rewrite wasn't the best idea. The vast majority of the second edition is still relevant, so it would have been better if we could just publish what's new. We decided to try out a new format for Microsoft Press books: the supplement. This will be the first supplement Microsoft Press delivers. I'm really happy that we were able to make this work, and if it weren't for Devon, this wouldn't have happened.

Valerie Woolley, our Project Editor at Microsoft Press, was critical to the delivery of this book. She has helped us stay on track with our deliverables and ensure that things keep moving. Thanks for keeping us on track, Valerie, and I apologize for not turning in all my content on the dates you requested.

In addition to the people that I have listed here there are several others who contributed to this book. With any significant project there are names that go unknown. I truly appreciate all the efforts of everyone involved in this book. I wish that I could name them all here. Thank you.

Last but certainly not least, I'd like to thank all the readers. You guys have stuck by us for two editions. I appreciate all the support and kind words that have been expressed about the books. Because of your support, we were able to publish the second edition, as well as this supplement. Please continue to let us know how we are doing. Hopefully, you will enjoy this supplement as much as the second edition.

William Bartholomew

First, I'd like to thank my third-time co-author, Sayed, because without him, this book would not be as broad as it is. From Microsoft Press, I'd like to thank Devon Musgrave, Valerie Woolley, and the art team for their efforts (and tolerance) in converting our ideas into a publishable book. Thanks must go to Marc Young for his technical review efforts in ensuring that the procedures are easily followed, the samples work, and the book makes sense. Finally, I'd like to thank the Team Build Team, in particular Justin Pinnix and Patrick Carnahan, for their tireless support.

Errata & book support

We've made every effort to ensure the accuracy of this book and its companion content. Any errors that have been reported since this book was published are listed on our Microsoft Press site at oreilly.com:

http://aka.ms/MSBuild2ESupp/errata

If you find an error that is not already listed, you can report it to us through the same page.

If you need additional support, email Microsoft Press Book Support at mspinput@microsoft.com.

Please note that product support for Microsoft software is not offered through the addresses above.

We want to hear from you

At Microsoft Press, your satisfaction is our top priority, and your feedback our most valuable asset. Please tell us what you think of this book at

http://aka.ms/tellpress

The survey is short, and we read every one of your comments and ideas. Thanks in advance for your input!

Stay in touch

Let's keep the conversation going! We're on Twitter: *http://twitter.com/MicrosoftPress*.

CHAPTER 1

What's new in MSBuild 4.5

The latest version of MSBuild is 4.5, which was released along with Microsoft .NET Framework 4.5 and Microsoft Visual Studio 2012. Typically, someone thinking of MSBuild includes items that are not technically a part of MSBuild. For example, it's very common to include updates to the build process or the web build and publish process for Visual Studio projects as a part of MSBuild. In reality, this support is built on top of MSBuild. With the release of .NET Framework 4.5 and Visual Studio 2012, you'll find many updates to pieces surrounding MSBuild, but only a few updates to the core MSBuild technology itself. In this chapter, we'll cover updates to MSBuild, as well as related technologies that you might already categorize as being part of MSBuild.

Visual Studio project compatibility between 2010 and 2012

One of the most requested features, if not *the* most requested feature, of Visual Studio 2012 was the ability to open a solution in Visual Studio 2012 while maintaining the ability for users to continue development with Visual Studio 2010 as well. This has been a common request for several versions of Visual Studio. With the 2012 release, this is now supported. With a few exceptions, you can have developers working on the same solution in either Visual Studio 2010 SP1 or Visual Studio 2012. This will enable a subset of your team to try out Visual Studio 2012 without requiring the entire team to upgrade overnight. Let's talk about what changes were required to accomplish this and what you need to know about it.

The solution file (*.sln*) has always had a file format version number built into it. The file format version for Visual Studio 2010 is 11.0, whereas for 2012 it is 12.0. Prior to Visual Studio 2010 SP1, if you opened an *.sln* file with a file format higher than what was expected, the solution would not be opened. In 2010 SP1, that behavior was relaxed. If 2010 SP1 is used to open an *.sln* file with the file format of 12.0, the file will be allowed to open. If the projects within that solution are supported with 2010, then they will be opened; otherwise, they will be left unloaded.

When you open an *.sln* file in Visual Studio 2012, there are three different possible outcomes:

- All projects are opened without any changes.

- One or more changes are required to make the projects compatible with both Visual Studio 2010 SP1 and 2012.

- One or more projects are left unloaded due to lack of support.

For the most part, your solutions should fall into the first category. The difference between the first and second options are that changes are required to one or more projects to ensure that they can be loaded by both versions. A good example of this are web projects. If you have a web project created with Visual Studio 2010, it will be modified slightly when it's first opened in Visual Studio 2012. The project will be modified to use a property for the location of the related *.targets* file instead of a hard-coded value. For the third case, there are some projects that 2012 no longer supports, so you will not be able to load those. For example, 2012 no longer supports Setup and Deployment projects, Extensibility projects for 2010, Web Deployment projects, and a few others. A new property, *VisualStudioVersion,* was introduced to assist in scenarios where multiple versions of Visual Studio may be used for a given project. Let's discuss this new property now.

VisualStudioVersion property

One of the enablers of sharing projects between Visual Studio 2010 and 2012 was the introduction of a new MSBuild property, *VisualStudioVersion*. When a project is built in Visual Studio, or from a developer command prompt, this property will be set to 11.0 or 10.0 for 2012 and 2010 SP1, respectively. One example of how this property is used can be found in the web project file. If you open the *.csproj/.vbproj* file of a web project, you will see these elements:

```
<PropertyGroup>
  <VisualStudioVersion Condition="'$(VisualStudioVersion)' == ''">10.0</VisualStudioVersion>
  <VSToolsPath
      Condition="'$(VSToolsPath)' == ''">
          $(MSBuildExtensionsPath32)\Microsoft\VisualStudio\v$(VisualStudioVersion)
  </VSToolsPath>
</PropertyGroup>
<Import Project="$(MSBuildBinPath)\Microsoft.CSharp.targets" />
<Import Project="$(VSToolsPath)\WebApplications\Microsoft.WebApplication.targets"
        Condition="'$(VSToolsPath)' != ''" />
<Import Project=
"$(MSBuildExtensionsPath32)\Microsoft\VisualStudio\v10.0\WebApplications\Microsoft.
WebApplication.targets"
        Condition="false" />
```

Here, you can see that the *VisualStudioVersion* property is initialized to 10.0 if it is not defined already. That property is used to determine the path to the Microsoft.WebApplication.targets file that is imported. Web projects created with 2010 previously hard-coded this value. By using the *VisualStudioVersion* property, these projects can be opened in either Visual Studio 2010 or 2012.

> **Note** You might have noticed the last import, which has v10.0 with a hard-coded
> Condition="false" code. Believe it or not, this is by design. Without this import, Visual
> Studio 2010 would treat the project as if it were out of date and "update" it by reinserting
> the import for the v10.0 targets file. To keep this from happening, the import cannot be
> removed.

When you are building solutions or projects from the command line, you should be aware of this property and know how it might affect your builds. First, let's cover how this property is being set, as it is not a reserved property. This property is set in the following way:

1. If *VisualStudioVersion* is defined as an environment variable or global MSBuild property, that is used as the value of this property.

2. If building an *.sln* file, the value used will equal `Solution File Format Version - 1`.

3. Choose a default: 10.0 if Visual Studio 2010 is installed, or else the value will be the highest version of the sub-toolset that is installed.

When you open a Visual Studio 2012 developer command prompt, *VisualStudioVersion* is defined as a global MSBuild property, so it is always available. If you are building *.sln* files from the command line, then you shouldn't have to worry about setting this property, but if you are building the project files, then you should set this value to ensure that there are no inconsistent behaviors from one machine to another. When building web projects specifically, you should always pass the correct value for *VisualStudioVersion*. For example, when building a web project using the build tools delivered with 2012, you can call Msbuild.exe in the following way:

```
msbuild.exe myproject.csproj /p:VisualStudioVersion=11.0
```

By invoking Msbuild.exe and passing in *VisualStudioVersion* as a command-line parameter, the property is declared as a global property. Because global properties have the highest priority, you can be sure that this value will be used. If you are using the MSBuild task to build a project, then you can pass the property into the *Properties* attribute. Now that we have covered Visual Studio compatibility, let's discuss some new ways that you can invoke tasks.

Out-of-process tasks

In MSBuild 4.0, it was difficult to invoke a task under a different context than the one that the build was executing in. For example, suppose you have a .NET task that needs to execute under a specific CPU architecture. In the past, you would have to be a bit creative to ensure that it was executed in the correct context. The task execution would be the same as the Msbuild.exe process. There are two different versions of Msbuild.exe: a 32-bit version and a 64-bit version. If you executed your build using the 32-bit version, then your task would be loaded in a 32-bit context, and the same goes for 64-bit.

In MSBuild 4.5, it's a lot easier to ensure that your tasks are loaded in the correct context. Two updates in MSBuild 4.5 enable this: new parameters for the *UsingTask* element and *Phantom Task* parameters. Let's start with the updates to the *UsingTask* declaration.

UsingTask updates

In the previous edition of this book, we showed many different examples of using tasks inside MSBuild project files, and we detailed the attributes of *UsingTask* in Chapter 4, "Custom tasks." The two new attributes that have been added in MSBuild 4.5 are listed in Table 1-1. When these attributes are present, they will affect all invocations when that task is loaded.

TABLE 1-1 New attributes of *UsingTask*

Attribute name	Description
Architecture	Sets the platform and architecture and bitness. The allowed values are *x86*, *x64*, *CurrentArchitecture*, or * for any of them.
Runtime	Sets the Common Language Runtime (CLR) version for the task context. Allowed values are *CLR2*, *CLR4*, *CurrentRuntime*, or * for any of them.

For example, if you have a task that requires that it always be executed under a 64-bit architecture, you would add the attribute *Architecture="x64"* to the *UsingTask* declaration. Without this, if the build was executed with the 64-bit version of Msbuild.exe (which can be found under %Windir%\Framework64\), then you would be OK, but if the 32-bit version (which can be found under %Windir%\Framework\), you would encounter errors. Let's see this in action.

Let's create a task that we can use as an example. We won't go over the details of how to create a task here. If you need a refresher, visit Chapter 4 in the previous edition. In the following snippet, you'll see the definition of the PrintInfo task:

```
using Microsoft.Build.Utilities;

public class PrintInfo : Task {

    public string Bitness {
        get {
            if (System.IntPtr.Size == 8) {
                return "64 bit";
            }

            return "32 bit";
        }
    }

    public string ClrVersion {
        get {
            return System.Environment.Version.ToString();
        }
    }


    public override bool Execute() {
        this.Log.LogMessage(
            ".NET CLR version: {0}\tBitness: {1}",
            this.ClrVersion,
            this.Bitness);
```

```
        return true;
    }
}
```

You can find this task in the samples that accompany this book. First, let's look at the default behavior when invoking this. The next code fragment shows the contents of Print-info-01.proj:

```xml
<Project ToolsVersion="4.0" DefaultTargets="Demo"
         xmlns="http://schemas.microsoft.com/developer/msbuild/2003">

  <UsingTask TaskName="PrintInfo"
    AssemblyFile="$(MSBuildThisFileDirectory)\BuildOutput\Samples.Ch01.dll"/>

  <Target Name="Demo">
    <PrintInfo />
  </Target>
</Project>
```

Now let's take a look at the result when this task is executed. From a Visual Studio 2012 Developer command prompt, execute the command `msbuild print-info-01.proj`. The result is shown in Figure 1-1.

```
C:\InsideMSBuild\ch01>msbuild print-info-01.proj /nologo
Build started 12/15/2012 7:58:06 PM.
Project "C:\InsideMSBuild\ch01\print-info-01.proj" on node 1 (default targets).
Demo:
  .NET CLR version: 4.0.30319.18010     Bitness: 32 bit
Done Building Project "C:\InsideMSBuild\ch01\print-info-01.proj" (default targe
```

FIGURE 1-1 The default result when building print-info-01.proj.

Here, you can see that the task is running under CLR 4.0, in a 32-bit context. You may be wondering why it's not running in a 64-bit context. Because we did not specify the architecture on the *UsingTask* declaration, the task is loaded in the context in which the build is executing. So it inherits the architecture of Msbuild.exe. In this case, we have invoked the 32-bit Msbuild.exe. The Visual Studio 2012 Developer command prompt will use the 32-bit version of Msbuild.exe by default. Now let's invoke it with the 64-bit version of Msbuild.exe and see the result. To make this simple, in the Visual Studio 2012 Developer command prompt, I created an alias to this executable using doskey msbuild64=%windir%\Microsoft.NET\Framework64\v4.0.30319\msbuild.exe $*. In Figure 1-2, you can see the result of running `msbuild64 print-info-01.proj`.

```
C:\InsideMSBuild\ch01>msbuild64 /nologo print-info-01.proj
Build started 12/15/2012 8:18:48 PM.
Project "C:\InsideMSBuild\ch01\print-info-01.proj" on node 1 (default targets).
Demo:
  .NET CLR version: 4.0.30319.18010     Bitness: 64 bit
Done Building Project "C:\InsideMSBuild\ch01\print-info-01.proj" (default targe
```

FIGURE 1-2 The result when building print-info-01.proj with the 64-bit version of Msbuild.exe.

In Figure 1-2, you can see that the PrintInfo task is now executed in a 64-bit context. If you need a task to load with a specific architecture or CLR run time, you can tweak the *UsingTask* element to indicate this. In the following code snippet, you will see the contents of Print-info-02.proj, which is very similar to the previous sample:

```xml
<Project ToolsVersion="4.0" DefaultTargets="Demo"
         xmlns="http://schemas.microsoft.com/developer/msbuild/2003">

  <PropertyGroup>
    <PrintInfoArch Condition="'$(PrintInfoArch)'==''">x86</PrintInfoArch>
  </PropertyGroup>

  <UsingTask TaskName="PrintInfo"
    Architecture="$(PrintInfoArch)"
    AssemblyFile="$(MSBuildThisFileDirectory)\BuildOutput\Samples.Ch01.dll"/>

  <Target Name="Demo">
    <Message Text="PrintInfoArch: $(PrintInfoArch)" />
    <PrintInfo />
  </Target>
</Project>
```

Here, you can see that a new property, *PrintInfoArch,* has been added. The default value for this property is *x86*. The value of this property is passed in as the value for the *Architecture* parameter on the *UsingTask* element. This will ensure that the task is always loaded with the specified architecture. Let's take a look at the result. In Figure 1-3, you will see the result of executing `msbuild.exe print-info-02.proj /p:PrintInfoArch=x64`.

```
C:\InsideMSBuild\ch01>msbuild print-info-02.proj /nologo /p:PrintInfoArch=x86
Build started 12/15/2012 8:32:35 PM.
Project "C:\InsideMSBuild\ch01\print-info-02.proj" on node 1 (default targets).
Demo:
  PrintInfoArch: x86
  .NET CLR version: 4.0.30319.18010    Bitness: 32 bit
Done Building Project "C:\InsideMSBuild\ch01\print-info-02.proj" (default target
```

FIGURE 1-3 The result when building Print-info-02.proj and specifying an x64 architecture.

Even though we are using the 32-bit version of Msbuild.exe, the task is loaded under a 64-bit context. You can use the *Runtime* attribute on *UsingTask* to load a task specifically under CLR 2.0 or CLR 4.0.

In the samples, you will find a few different varieties of the PrintInfo task. Each class contains the same code, but the containing project targets a different run time/architecture. The sample shown here, taken from Print-info-03-v2.proj, shows how we can ensure that the PrintInfo task is loaded with CLR 2:

```xml
<Project ToolsVersion="4.0" DefaultTargets="Demo"
         xmlns="http://schemas.microsoft.com/developer/msbuild/2003">

  <UsingTask TaskName="PrintInfo"
    Runtime="CLR2"
    AssemblyFile="$(MSBuildThisFileDirectory)\BuildOutput\Samples.Ch01.v2.dll"/>
```

```
   <Target Name="Demo">
     <PrintInfo />
   </Target>
</Project>
```

Here, we pass *CLR2* as the *Runtime* attribute value. Similarly, we can ensure that it's loaded under CLR 4.0 with the following code from Print-info-03-v4.proj:

```
<Project ToolsVersion="4.0" DefaultTargets="Demo"
         xmlns="http://schemas.microsoft.com/developer/msbuild/2003">

  <UsingTask TaskName="PrintInfo"
     Runtime="CLR4"
     AssemblyFile="$(MSBuildThisFileDirectory)\BuildOutput\Samples.Ch01.v4.dll"/>

  <Target Name="Demo">
     <PrintInfo />
  </Target>
</Project>
```

The results of building all these project files are shown in Figure 1-4.

```
C:\InsideMSBuild\ch01>msbuild print-info-03-v2.proj /nologo
Build started 12/16/2012 2:15:05 PM.
Project "C:\InsideMSBuild\ch01\print-info-03-v2.proj" on node 1 (default targets
Demo:
   .NET CLR version: 2.0.50727.6400     Bitness: 32 bit
Done Building Project "C:\InsideMSBuild\ch01\print-info-03-v2.proj" (default tar


C:\InsideMSBuild\ch01>msbuild print-info-03-v4.proj /nologo
Build started 12/16/2012 2:15:10 PM.
Project "C:\InsideMSBuild\ch01\print-info-03-v4.proj" on node 1 (default targets
Demo:
   .NET CLR version: 4.0.30319.18010    Bitness: 32 bit
Done Building Project "C:\InsideMSBuild\ch01\print-info-03-v4.proj" (default tar
```

FIGURE 1-4 The result showing the PrintInfo task loaded under CLR 2.0 and then CLR 4.0.

Figure 1-4 demonstrates that we were able to load a task successfully under a specific .NET CLR version. We have seen how to control the context in which a task gets loaded by modifying the *UsingTask* attribute. What may not be entirely obvious at this point is that you can actually load different versions of the same task. You can use a couple of new attributes on the task to indicate which version should be picked up automatically. Let's see how this works.

Phantom task parameters

From the previous edition, you know that a task can contain any number of inputs and outputs. All those inputs and outputs would be passed in using attributes of the task itself. With MSBuild 4.5, two new attributes are allowed for task invocations: *MSBuildRuntime* and *MSBuildArchitecture*. These parameters control the context in which the task is loaded and are not actually passed to the task itself. The task is not aware of the presence of these parameters, and there is no way to detect their presence (the task itself can determine the execution context in code if needed). This is why they are called *phantom task parameters*.

Suppose that you have a task that has been implemented for both CLR 2.0 and CLR 4.0. How could you use both these tasks in the same MSBuild script? To keep things simple, I have created a SayHello task which has four slightly different implementations, depending on which architecture or version of the CLR it supports. In the following code block, you will find the implementation for the CLR 4.0 version of the task:

```
using Microsoft.Build.Utilities;

public class SayHello : Task {
    public override bool Execute() {
        Log.LogMessage("Hello using .NET CLR 4");
        return true;
    }
}
```

The other implementations of the task are similar. In the code snippet that follows, you will find the contents of the file Say-hello-01.proj:

```
<Project ToolsVersion="4.0" DefaultTargets="Demo"
        xmlns="http://schemas.microsoft.com/developer/msbuild/2003">

  <UsingTask TaskName="SayHello"
    Runtime="CLR2"
    AssemblyFile="$(MSBuildThisFileDirectory)BuildOutput\Samples.Ch01.v2.dll"/>

  <UsingTask TaskName="SayHello"
    Runtime="CLR4"
    AssemblyFile="$(MSBuildThisFileDirectory)BuildOutput\Samples.Ch01.v4.dll"/>

  <Target Name="Demo">
    <SayHello MSBuildRuntime="CLR2"/>
    <SayHello MSBuildRuntime="CLR4"/>

    <SayHello />
  </Target>
</Project>
```

In this sample, you can see that we are loading two versions of the SayHello task. One is built targeting .NET CLR 2.0, and the other invokes .NET CLR 4.0. In the Demo target, we can see three invocations of the SayHello task. The last one does not pass any parameters, and the first two specify the value for MSBuildRuntime. First, let's take a look at the result and then delve into the details. You can see the result of building this project in Figure 1-5.

```
C:\InsideMSBuild\ch01>msbuild say-hello-01.proj /nologo
Build started 12/16/2012 2:21:05 PM.
Project "C:\InsideMSBuild\ch01\say-hello-01.proj" on node 1 (default targets).
Demo:
  Hello using .NET CLR 2
  Hello using .NET CLR 4
  Hello using .NET CLR 2
Done Building Project "C:\InsideMSBuild\ch01\say-hello-01.proj" (default targets
```

FIGURE 1-5 The result of building Say-hello-01.proj.

Here, you can see that, as expected, the correct version of the task was invoked based on the *MSBuildRuntime* value for the first two invocations. From the message displayed from the third invocation, it is clear that the CLR 2.0 version of the task is invoked. When MSBuild encounters a task invocation inside a target, it will use the following information to find the corresponding task: the task name, *MSBuildRuntime* value, and *MSBuildArchitecture* value. It will search through all the available tasks (those that have been registered with *UsingTask*) and find the first task that meets the criteria. In the previous sample, when <SayHello MSBuildRuntime="CLR2" /> is encountered, MSBuild will return the task declared in the first *UsingTask*, which is Runtime="CLR2". If there is no *UsingTask* declaration with Runtime="CLR2", then the first SayHello task is returned. In our case, the first *UsingTask* declaration indicated Runtime="CLR2", so that one was loaded when <SayHello /> is encountered. If we had defined the Runtime="CLR4" *UsingTask* declaration first, then that version would have been loaded instead. In the samples, you can find Say-hello-02.proj, which demonstrates this case. Now let's take a look at something new: a package manager called *NuGet*.

NuGet

When you are developing an application, the odds are that you will be reusing components created by others. For example, you would like to add logging to your application. Instead of writing your own logging framework, it would be much easier to use one of the existing ones out there, such as log4net or NLog. In the past, you would typically have integrated external dependencies in your application by following these basic steps:

1. Find the developer's website and download binaries.

2. Add one or more references to these binaries in Visual Studio.

3. Copy and paste sample code from the website into your project.

After that, you would have to update those references manually. *NuGet* makes this process much simpler.

NuGet is available from its home page, *nuget.org,* as well as the Visual Studio gallery. On the *NuGet* extension page in the Visual Studio gallery, *NuGet* is described as "A collection of tools to automate the process of downloading, installing, upgrading, configuring, and removing packages from a VS Project." Essentially, *NuGet* is a package manager for Visual Studio projects. A package is a self-contained unit that can be installed into a project. *NuGet* packages can do all sorts of things, including adding references, adding code files, and modifying Web.config. *NuGet* is integrated with Visual Studio 2012, but it is available for Visual Studio 2010 as well.

Managing *NuGet* packages

In this scenario, integrating a logging framework into your project using *NuGet* requires just one step. You simply need to install the *NuGet* package for the logging framework you want. You do not need to know the developer's web address or which references need to be added. In many cases, if an update is required for Web.config or App.config, the *NuGet* package will make those changes as well.

There are two ways to add a *NuGet* package to a project: using the Manage NuGet Packages dialog box or the Package Manager Console. We will describe both methods next.

You can open the Manage NuGet Packages dialog box by right-clicking a project in Solution Explorer and selecting Manage NuGet Packages. You will see the dialog box shown in Figure 1-6.

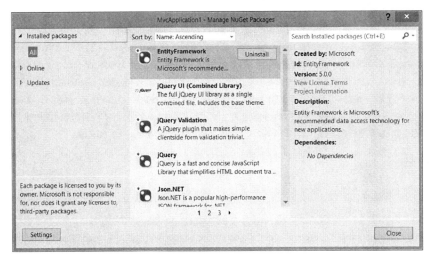

FIGURE 1-6 The Manage NuGet Packages dialog box.

The installed packages will vary based on your project. For example, if you open this dialog box for a default C# Class Library project, the list will be empty. C# class libraries do not add any *NuGet* packages by default, but some other project types do. From this dialog box, you can manage your *NuGet* packages. You can find new packages on the Online tab. You can use the search bar on the right to locate specific packages. For example, Figure 1-7 displays the results when I searched for "log4net" while looking at the Online tab.

FIGURE 1-7 The search results for "log4net" in the Manage NuGet Packages dialog box.

To install the selected package, you simply click Install. Then the package will be downloaded and installed into your project automatically. *NuGet* packages can depend on other packages. If the package being installed depends on other packages, they will be installed automatically as well.

When a package is installed for the first time into a project, a few things happen:

- A Packages folder is created in the solution directory.

- A Packages.config file is dropped into the project's folder.

- The package is installed into the project.

The Packages folder contains the downloaded packages. The Packages.config file is an XML file that lists all the installed *NuGet* packages for a given project. The Packages folder contains a folder for each package. These packages are shared across the entire solution. If a package contains any assemblies that will be added as a reference, they will be placed inside the folder for that particular package. Typically, you do not want to check in the Packages folder, so we need a way to download those packages on demand. This is where package restore comes in. We will cover package restore in the "Package Restore" section later in this chapter, after we discuss managing packages.

In this same dialog box, you also can update packages. If you open the Manage NuGet Packages dialog box, you can see what packages have updates by clicking the Updates tab. For example, in Figure 1-8, you can see that the selected project has two *NuGet* packages with updates available.

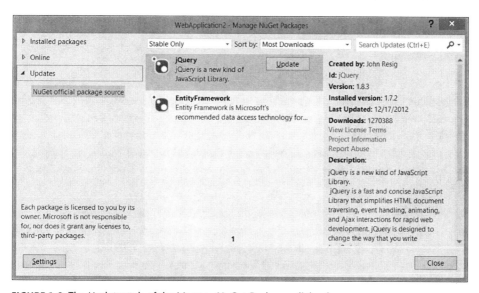

FIGURE 1-8 The Updates tab of the Manage NuGet Packages dialog box.

To update a selected package, you simply click Update. You can also use the Install Packages tab to uninstall packages. Simply click the Uninstall button on the selected package itself. Earlier we mentioned that you can also manage *NuGet* packages in the Package Manager Console. Let's take a look at that experience.

Package Manager Console

To access the Package Manager Console, we need to first load the window. To do this, from the View menu, go to Other Windows and select Package Manager Console. Then you will see the console shown in Figure 1-9.

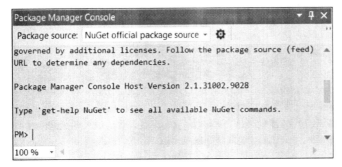

FIGURE 1-9 The Package Manager Console in Visual Studio.

This prompt is actually a Windows PowerShell prompt with the *NuGet* functionality already loaded. You can issue any Windows PowerShell command, but there are a few *NuGet*-specific commands as well. For example, you can execute the following commands:

- Install-Package

- Uninstall-Package

- Update-Package

To see the full list of *NuGet*-specific commands, simply execute get-help NuGet. Because this is a Windows PowerShell prompt, you get all the benefits of using a Windows PowerShell prompt, including statement completion, piping of commands, and object inspection. Because of this, you do not need to memorize all the parameters for the Install-Package command. You can simply press Tab to be shown a list of the parameters. The simplest command to install a package is Install-Package <package-name>. For example, to install Modernizr, execute Install-Package Modernizr.

Using the Package Manager Console, you have more control over package management. For example, you can install a specific version of a package from the console. At this time, the latest released version of the Entity Framework NuGet package is 5.0.0. If you needed to install the 4.3.1 version, you can execute the command Install-Package EntityFramework -Version 4.3.1. Note that when browsing packages at *nuget.org*, you will find the command required to install that specific package.

Package Restore

Because it's recommended that you do not check in the Packages folder (after all, you don't want a bunch of binaries clogging your repository), there is an additional step that needs to be taken before checking in a project using NuGet. You need to enable Package Restore. After this is enabled, when the project is built it will automatically download the packages as needed. To enable Package Restore, right-click the solution in Solution Explorer and select Enable NuGet Package Restore.

> **Note** Alternatively, you can install nuget.exe in a well-known location on your build server and use that for Package Restore. This would prevent you from checking in several different copies of nuget.exe for each solution. We won't cover that here, though.

When you enable package restore on a given solution, a few things happen:

- A .nuget folder is created with the required files, including Nuget.targets.

- The solution is updated to show these files in a solution folder.

- Each project with *NuGet* packages is updated to import the Nuget.targets file.

After package restore has been enabled, the missing *NuGet* packages will be downloaded automatically each time the solution or project is built. Enabling package restore is essentially a requirement for team scenarios. Because package restore is implemented using MSBuild, the package restore functionality will be invoked automatically when your project is built from Visual Studio, the command line, or a build server. Let's take a closer look at the package restore process.

After enabling package restore, if you open the *.csproj/.vbproj* file, you will find the Import statement `<Import Project="$(SolutionDir)\.nuget\nuget.targets" />`. This MSBuild *.targets* file defines the RestorePackages target. This target is injected into the build process using the following property declaration:

```
<!-- We need to ensure packages are restored prior to assembly resolve -->
<ResolveReferencesDependsOn Condition="$(RestorePackages) == 'true'">
    RestorePackages;
    $(ResolveReferencesDependsOn);
</ResolveReferencesDependsOn>
```

If the *RestorePackages* property is set to *True,* then the RestorePackages target will be executed before the references are resolved for a given project. The RestorePackages target does not restore the packages; rather, it calls Nuget.exe to do this. Nuget.exe will examine the Packages.config file and restore the missing packages. Nuget.exe is one of the files that are placed in the .nuget folder when package restore is enabled. In the following code block, you can see how the RestorePackages target is defined:

```
<Target Name="RestorePackages" DependsOnTargets="CheckPrerequisites">
    <Exec Command="$(RestoreCommand)"
          Condition="'$(OS)' != 'Windows_NT' And Exists('$(PackagesConfig)')" />

    <Exec Command="$(RestoreCommand)"
          LogStandardErrorAsError="true"
          Condition="'$(OS)' == 'Windows_NT' And Exists('$(PackagesConfig)')" />
</Target>
```

After the execution of this target, all the required assembly references will have been downloaded into the Packages folder, and your build happily continues. For more details on the package restore process, take a look at the NuGet.targets file. Now that we have covered NuGet, we will take a look at another useful Visual Studio extension.

XML updates with SlowCheetah

Have you ever been developing an application that targeted different environments and wish you had an easy way to debug your application with different settings? In the past, when I found myself in this situation, I would have to update App.config manually with the environment that I wanted to debug. After debugging the environment, I would have to remember to roll back my settings. This is a painful, error-prone way to solve this problem. It would be great if there were a way to do this automatically when you use F5 in Visual Studio.

A relatively new Visual Studio extension, SlowCheetah, allows you to do exactly that. SlowCheetah is available for both Visual Studio 2010 and Visual Studio 2012. It uses XML Document Transforms (XDTs), also known as Web.config transforms, to execute the transformations. In Chapter 18 of the previous edition, "Web Deployment Tool, Part 2," we showed how to create Web.config transforms. We also covered all the details on creating XDTs. If you need to brush up on XDT syntax, take a look back at that chapter. SlowCheetah is available for download at the Visual Studio gallery (*http://visualstudiogallery.msdn.microsoft.com/69023d00-a4f9-4a34-a6cd-7e854ba318b5*). The project is open-source. For more info on SlowCheetah, visit *http://msbuildbook.com/slowcheetah*.

For web projects, the Web.config transforms are invoked during a publish or package operation. They are not executed during build (F5). This is the default behavior for web projects. SlowCheetah may be able to invoke the transforms on F5 for web projects, but that support is not implemented yet.

For non-web projects, after installing SlowCheetah, you can add an App.config transform by right-clicking app.config and selecting Add Transform. Once you do this, you will see a transform file for each project build configuration. In Figure 1-10, you can see the result for a project that only has Debug and Release defined.

FIGURE 1-10 The Add Transform result for a project with two build configurations.

After this, each time you build your application, the App.config file will be transformed with the appropriate App.*xxx*.config transform. This is true if you are building in Visual Studio or from the command line. Let's see how this works.

In the samples accompanying this book, you will find a console project file, TransformSample .Console.csproj, which uses SlowCheetah. You will need to have installed SlowCheetah for this sample to work correctly. This project will read the application's configuration file and output the application settings to the console. Since the App.config file will be updated during build (or F5 in Visual Studio), this application should output different values when the build configuration is switched. Let's take a look at the App.config file for this project, shown in Listing 1-1.

LISTING 1-1 App.config file contents

```xml
<?xml version="1.0" encoding="utf-8" ?>
<configuration>
  <appSettings>
    <add key="appName" value="console-default"/>
    <add key="url" value="http://localhost:8080/"/>
    <add key="email" value="default@localhost.com"/>
  </appSettings>

  <connectionStrings configSource="connectionStrings.config" />

</configuration>
```

The App.config file here is very basic; it just includes a few application settings. The connection strings are loaded from another file. These are the values that the application would normally be loaded with. Now let's take a look at the transforms. Listing 1-2 shows the contents of the App.Debug. config transform.

LISTING 1-2 App.Debug.config contents

```xml
<configuration xmlns:xdt="http://schemas.microsoft.com/XML-Document-Transform">

  <appSettings>
    <add key="appName" value="Demo-Debug"
         xdt:Transform="Replace" xdt:Locator="Match(key)"/>

    <add key="url" value="http://debug:8080/"
         xdt:Transform="Replace" xdt:Locator="Match(key)"/>

    <add key="email" value="debug@contoso.com"
         xdt:Transform="Replace" xdt:Locator="Match(key)"/>
  </appSettings>

</configuration>
```

From the previous listing, you can see that XDT is being used to update the three appSettings entries when the project is built using Debug mode. Similarly, the App.Release.config file updates these entries as well, as shown in Listing 1-3.

LISTING 1-3 App.Release.config contents

```xml
<configuration xmlns:xdt="http://schemas.microsoft.com/XML-Document-Transform">

  <appSettings>
    <add key="appName" value="Demo-Release"
         xdt:Transform="Replace" xdt:Locator="Match(key)"/>

    <add key="url" value="http://contoso.com/"
         xdt:Transform="Replace" xdt:Locator="Match(key)"/>
```

```
    <add key="email" value="release@contoso.com"
        xdt:Transform="Replace" xdt:Locator="Match(key)"/>
  </appSettings>

</configuration>
```

Let's see what happens when we run this application in Debug and Release mode. In Figure 1-11, you can see the result when the application is run in Debug mode, and Figure 1-12 has the results for Release mode.

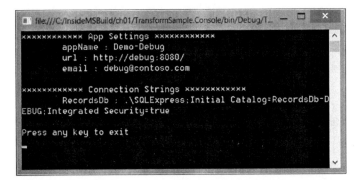

FIGURE 1-11 The TransformSample result when running in Debug mode.

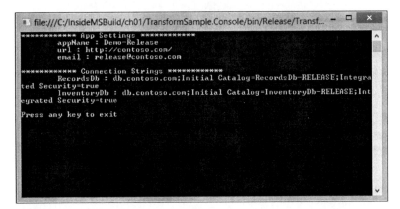

FIGURE 1-12 The TransformSample result when running in Release mode.

In these two images, we can see that the three application settings (appName, url, and email) are updated automatically when we hit F5 in Visual Studio. You can see that the connection strings are updated as well. Because the *connectionStrings* element includes configSource="connectionStrings.config", the values for connection strings will be taken from ConnectionStrings.config. This file is also transformed with SlowCheetah. When using SlowCheetah, you are not limited to transforming App.config; it can transform any XML file. The extension of the file does not have to be .*config*. We will not discuss the transformation for ConnectionString.config here, but you can find it in the samples. Now that we are familiar with the transformations, let's take a look at how we can invoke them on a build server.

SlowCheetah build server support

SlowCheetah build server support can easily be implemented with the help of the SlowCheetah *NuGet* package. This package is installed automatically the first time that you invoke the Add Transform menu option. Let's take a look at how SlowCheetah integrates into your projects, and then we will discuss how to set up your build servers.

When the SlowCheetah package is installed, the following elements are added to your project file:

```
<PropertyGroup Label="SlowCheetah">
  <SlowCheetah_EnableImportFromNuGet
    Condition=" '$(SlowCheetah_EnableImportFromNuGet)'=='' ">
    true</SlowCheetah_EnableImportFromNuGet>

  <SlowCheetah_NuGetImportPath
    Condition=" '$(SlowCheetah_NuGetImportPath)'=='' ">
    $([System.IO.Path]::GetFullPath(
      $(MSBuildProjectDirectory)\.\packages\
        SlowCheetah.2.5.5.1\tools\SlowCheetah.Transforms.targets ))
  </SlowCheetah_NuGetImportPath>

  <SlowCheetahTargets
    Condition=" '$(SlowCheetah_EnableImportFromNuGet)'=='true' and
      Exists('$(SlowCheetah_NuGetImportPath)') ">
    $(SlowCheetah_NuGetImportPath)
  </SlowCheetahTargets>
</PropertyGroup>

<!-- Other project elements will appear between these -->

<Import Project="$(SlowCheetahTargets)" Condition="Exists('$(SlowCheetahTargets)')"
        Label="SlowCheetah" />
```

The property *SlowCheetahTargets* will be populated with the location of the *.targets* file that will be imported. Next to the *.targets* file is an assembly that contains the TransformXml MSBuild task. This is the task responsible for executing the transformations. Because these files are delivered using *NuGet*, for automated builds, we can employ Package Restore to download the needed files.

If you plan on executing builds from a build server, you should make sure to enable Package Restore on the solution.

When the package is installed, the following changes are applied:

- The required files are placed in the Packages folder.

- Your project is updated to load the *.targets* file from the Packages folder.

- A PackageRestore.proj file is created at the root of your project.

Now when you build your project, the *.targets* file will be imported from the Packages folder. As covered in the "Package Restore" section earlier in this chapter, a *NuGet* package that extends the build process needs to be restored before the build for your solution/project starts. This is where the

PackageRestore.proj file comes into play. If you open the PackageRestore.proj file, it will look like the following code block:

```
<Project ToolsVersion="4.0" DefaultTargets="RestorePackages"
         xmlns="http://schemas.microsoft.com/developer/msbuild/2003">

  <PropertyGroup>
    <SolutionDir
      Condition="$(SolutionDir) == '' Or $(SolutionDir) == '*Undefined*'"
      Label="SlowCheetahSolutionDir">..\</SolutionDir>
  </PropertyGroup>

  <Import Project="$(SolutionDir)\.nuget\nuget.targets" />
</Project>
```

> **Note** If you did not have Package Restore enabled when the package was installed, you should enable Package Restore and then manually uninstall and reinstall the SlowCheetah package.

This is a very basic MSBuild file. All it does is define the *SolutionDir* property and then import the Nuget.targets file. If this looks familiar, it's because this is the same type of edits that are made to your project file when you enable package restore. The PackageRestore.proj file itself does not do the work of restoring the packages; this is left to Nuget.targets. In order to restore your packages, you can execute the command `msbuild packageRestore.proj`. This will restore all the packages that your project utilizes. Let's see how we can configure Team Build for this scenario.

If you are using Team Build, it is very easy to build the PackageRestore.proj file before your solution/project is built. When configuring your build definition on the Process tab, you can select the items that will be built from the Items To Build list. You can see these items highlighted in Figure 1-13.

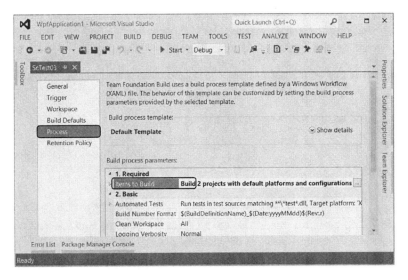

FIGURE 1-13 The Items To Build list on the Process tab.

When you edit the Items To Build list, you should add the PackageRestore.proj file to the list and make sure that it is at the top of the list (see Figure 1-14).

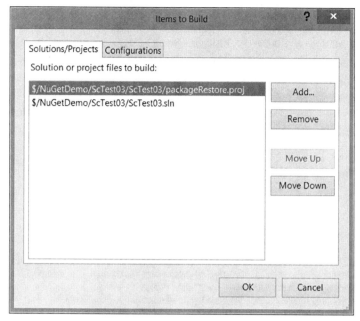

FIGURE 1-14 The Items To Build dialog box.

Because the PackageRestore.proj file is at the very top of the list, it will be built before the other items. Once this project is built, it will restore the necessary package and the transforms will be executed as expected on your build servers. That is all you need to enable the transformations to be executed on your build servers. Now that we have covered SlowCheetah, let's move on to the next section where we will do some hands-on experimentation.

Cookbook

This section presents instructions on how to implement and customize some of the new features in MSBuild 4.5.

How to extend the solution build

One of the most commonly asked questions is "How can I extend the build process for my solution?" It's easy to extend the build process for a project, but extending the *solution* build is an entirely different thing. It is possible to extend the solution build process from the command line, but not from within Visual Studio. The content in this answer relates to command-line builds only.

The *.sln* file is not an MSBuild file. MSBuild is able to build an *.sln* file, though. Because of this, we cannot use the techniques that we've already learned to execute additional targets. Before we get to the specific implementation, let's discuss what happens when Msbuild.exe builds an *.sln* file.

When MSBuild attempts to build an *.sln* file, it is first converted to an MSBuild file in memory. That is how MSBuild consumes the solution file. When building an *.sln* file at the command prompt, you can have MSBuild write out the MSBuild version of the *.sln* file. To do this, create the environment variable *MSBuildEmitSolution* and set it to 1. If you set this using the Environment Variables dialog box, you will need to reopen your command prompt before this change can take effect. With this environment variable present when you build an *.sln* file, two files will be generated in the same folder as the *.sln* file. Those two files are named {SolutionName}.sln.metaproj and {SolutionName}.sln. metaproj.tmp, and they can provide some insight into the process.

If you open the *.metaproj.tmp* file, you will see that the contents are roughly as shown in the next code segment:

```xml
<?xml version="1.0" encoding="utf-8"?>
<Project ToolsVersion="4.0" xmlns="http://schemas.microsoft.com/developer/msbuild/2003"
         DefaultTargets="Build"
         InitialTargets="ValidateSolutionConfiguration;ValidateToolsVersions;ValidateProjects">
  <Import Project="$(MSBuildExtensionsPath)\$(MSBuildToolsVersion)\SolutionFile\ImportBefore\*"
         Condition="'$(ImportByWildcardBeforeSolution)' != 'false'
         and exists('$(MSBuildExtensionsPath)\$(MSBuildToolsVersion)\SolutionFile\
ImportBefore')" />

  <Import Project="C:\InsideMSBuild\ch01\ExtendSlnBuild\before.ExtendSlnBuild.sln.targets"
         Condition="exists('C:\InsideMSBuild\ch01\ExtendSlnBuild\before.ExtendSlnBuild.sln.
targets')" />

  <!-- Properties/items removed from here -->

  <Import Project="$(MSBuildExtensionsPath)\$(MSBuildToolsVersion)\SolutionFile\ImportAfter\*"
         Condition="'$(ImportByWildcardBeforeSolution)' != 'false' and
         exists('$(MSBuildExtensionsPath)\$(MSBuildToolsVersion)\SolutionFile\ImportAfter')" />

  <Import Project="C:\InsideMSBuild\ch01\ExtendSlnBuild\after.ExtendSlnBuild.sln.targets"
         Condition="exists('C:\InsideMSBuild\ch01\ExtendSlnBuild\after.ExtendSlnBuild.sln.
targets')" />

  <!-- Targets removed -->
</Project>
```

Some irrelevant elements were removed from this code for the sake of space. In the *.metaproj .tmp* file, there are two pairs of *Import* statements: one pair at the top of the file, which imports MSBuild files before the content in the *.metaproj.tmp* file, and another pair at the bottom, which imports MSBuild files after the content. The difference between importing your MSBuild files before or after the content is subtle but important. When your file is imported before the *.metaproj.tmp* file's content, that means you will not be able to use any properties/items that are declared in the *.metaproj.tmp* file. The advantage of this approach is that it gives you a chance to set the properties/ items first. Typically, I default to importing my files by using one of the *after Import* statements. This way, I can use all the properties and items if needed.

In each pair of *Import* statements, the first *Import* uses the *$(MSBuildExtensionsPath)* property. The code snippet above the *Import* declaration in one case is $(MSBuildExtensionsPath)\$(MSBuildToolsVersion)\SolutionFile\ImportAfter*. On a 64-bit machine, this evaluates to C:\ Program Files (x86)\MSBuild\4.0\SolutionFile\ImportAfter* by default. If there are any files in this folder, they will be imported into the build process for every .*sln* file that is built from the command line using Msbuild.exe. This is a good solution for build servers, but it's also a bit heavy-handed. It affects every single build on that machine. Typically, it's preferred to have a more targeted solution. That is where the second *Import* element is used.

In the previous sample, the *Import* declaration from the bottom pair imports C:\InsideMSBuild\ ch01\ExtendSlnBuild\after.ExtendSlnBuild.sln.targets. The pattern here is that the .*targets* file is placed in the same folder as the .*sln* file and named after .*{SolutionName}*.sln.targets, where *{SolutionName}* is the name of the solution. This is the preferred method to extend the solution build.

Included with the samples is a solution named ExtendSlnBuild.sln. This sample contains a single project, ClassLibrary.csproj. In the same folder as ExtendSlnBuild.sln, there is a file called After.ExtendSlnBuild.sln.targets, which will be picked up and imported into the build process automatically. Let's take a look at the contents of that file and then discuss the details. The contents of After.ExtendSlnBuild.sln.targets are shown in the following code fragment:

```xml
<?xml version="1.0" encoding="utf-8"?>
<Project xmlns="http://schemas.microsoft.com/developer/msbuild/2003">

  <Target Name="GenerateCode" BeforeTargets="Build;Rebuild">
    <Message Text="**********************************" Importance="high"/>
    <Message Text="             Generate Code        " Importance="high"/>
    <Message Text="**********************************" Importance="high"/>
  </Target>

  <Target Name="AnalyzeCode" AfterTargets="Build;Rebuild">
    <Message Text="**********************************" Importance="high"/>
    <Message Text="             Analyze Code         " Importance="high"/>
    <Message Text="**********************************" Importance="high"/>
  </Target>

</Project>
```

In this MSBuild file, there are two targets: GenerateCode and AnalyzeCode. They will be executed before and after the solution build process, respectively. These targets are injected into the build process using the *BeforeTargets* and *AfterTargets* attributes. A solution file will always have the following four targets:

- Build

- Rebuild

- Clean

- Publish

For this example, we want to execute our targets whenever a build is occurring. You might have noticed in the sample that in the BeforeTargets/AfterTargets, the value was defined as *"Build;Rebuild"* instead of simply *Build*. The solution file does not attempt to interpret Build and Rebuild; it simply invokes the appropriate target on each project file. Because of this, when calling Rebuild on the solution, the Build target is not invoked on it. This is different from the typical case for project files. When you build the ExtendedSlnBuild.sln file from the command prompt, the result will be similar to Figure 1-15.

```
C:\InsideMSBuild\ch01\ExtendSlnBuild>msbuild ExtendSlnBuild.sln /nologo
Building the projects in this solution one at a time. To enable parallel bu
Build started 12/25/2012 8:59:03 PM.
Project "C:\InsideMSBuild\ch01\ExtendSlnBuild\ExtendSlnBuild.sln" on node 1
ValidateSolutionConfiguration:
  Building solution configuration "Debug|Any CPU".
GenerateCode:
    ××××××××××××××××××××××××××××××××××
             Generate Code
    ××××××××××××××××××××××××××××××××××
Project "C:\InsideMSBuild\ch01\ExtendSlnBuild\ExtendSlnBuild.sln" (1) is bu
lt targets).
GenerateTargetFrameworkMonikerAttribute:
Skipping target "GenerateTargetFrameworkMonikerAttribute" because all outpu
CoreCompile:
Skipping target "CoreCompile" because all output files are up-to-date with
CopyFilesToOutputDirectory:
  ClassLibrary -> C:\InsideMSBuild\ch01\ExtendSlnBuild\ClassLibrary\bin\Deb
Done Building Project "C:\InsideMSBuild\ch01\ExtendSlnBuild\ClassLibrary\Cl

AnalyzeCode:
    ××××××××××××××××××××××××××××××××××
             Analyze Code
    ××××××××××××××××××××××××××××××××××
Done Building Project "C:\InsideMSBuild\ch01\ExtendSlnBuild\ExtendSlnBuild.
```

FIGURE 1-15 The result of building ExtendSlnBuild.sln using Msbuild.exe.

In Figure 1-15, you can see that the GenerateCode target is executed before any project is built and the AnalyzeCode target is executed after all the projects in the solution have completed.

How to execute a target only if the project is actually built

In many cases, you may need to run a tool if, and only if, your output is rebuilt. For example, in a C# project, you might want a target to run only if the C# compiler is called. In general, this is not a straightforward task with MSBuild. But there is a special hook that we can use for this specific case. Before describing this, let's discuss the typical case and why it is so difficult.

Skipping of targets is handled by incremental building. In Chapter 6 of the previous edition, "Batching and Incremental Builds," we covered incremental building in detail. When a target is executed, if it has inputs and outputs, they will be examined to see if the target needs to be executed. The check is based on timestamps. If the timestamps of all the outputs have a later timestamp than the inputs, then the target will be skipped.

In the following sample, you will find the contents of Inc-build-01.proj:

```xml
<?xml version="1.0" encoding="utf-8"?>
<Project ToolsVersion="4.0" DefaultTargets="CopyFiles"
xmlns="http://schemas.microsoft.com/developer/msbuild/2003">
  <PropertyGroup>
    <OutputFolder>$(MSBuildProjectDirectory)\BuildOutput\incBuild\</OutputFolder>
  </PropertyGroup>

  <ItemGroup>
    <FilesToCopy Include="$(MSBuildProjectDirectory)\*.proj" />
  </ItemGroup>

  <Target Name="CopyFiles" Inputs="@(FilesToCopy)" Outputs="@(FilesToCopy->'$(OutputFolder)%
(Filename)%(Extension)')">
    <Copy SourceFiles="@(FilesToCopy)"
          DestinationFiles="@(FilesToCopy->'$(OutputFolder)%(Filename)%(Extension)')" />
  </Target>

  <Target Name="AfterCopyFiles" AfterTargets="CopyFiles">
    <Message Text="***** AfterCopyFiles target executing"/>
  </Target>

  <Target Name="Clean">
    <ItemGroup>
      <_FilesToDelete Include="$(OutputFolder)*.proj"/>
    </ItemGroup>
    <Delete Files="@(_FilesToDelete)"/>
  </Target>
</Project>
```

In this project file, we have just three targets defined. The CopyFiles target will copy a set of *.proj* files to the BuildOutput\IncBuild folder. The files to copy are placed in the FilesToCopy item list. The CopyFiles target has its inputs and outputs set up so that the target will be skipped if all the files are up to date. The AfterCopyFiles target will be executed after the CopyFiles. Let's take a look at the behavior when the BuildOutput\IncBuild folder is clean. The result of invoking Inc-build-01.proj in MSBuild is shown in Figure 1-16.

```
C:\InsideMSBuild\ch01>msbuild inc-build-01.proj /nologo
Build started 12/25/2012 9:50:13 PM.
Project "C:\InsideMSBuild\ch01\inc-build-01.proj" on node 1 (default targets).
CopyFiles:
  Copying file from "C:\InsideMSBuild\ch01\ch01.proj" to "C:\InsideMSBuild\ch01\BuildOutput\incB
  uild\ch01.proj".
  Copying file from "C:\InsideMSBuild\ch01\inc-build-01.proj" to "C:\InsideMSBuild\ch01\BuildOut
  put\incBuild\inc-build-01.proj".
  Copying file from "C:\InsideMSBuild\ch01\inc-build-02.proj" to "C:\InsideMSBuild\ch01\BuildOut
  put\incBuild\inc-build-02.proj".
  Copying file from "C:\InsideMSBuild\ch01\print-info-01.proj" to "C:\InsideMSBuild\ch01\BuildOu
  tput\incBuild\print-info-01.proj".
  Copying file from "C:\InsideMSBuild\ch01\print-info-02.proj" to "C:\InsideMSBuild\ch01\BuildOu
  tput\incBuild\print-info-02.proj".
  Copying file from "C:\InsideMSBuild\ch01\print-info-03-v2.proj" to "C:\InsideMSBuild\ch01\Buil
  dOutput\incBuild\print-info-03-v2.proj".
  Copying file from "C:\InsideMSBuild\ch01\print-info-03-v4.proj" to "C:\InsideMSBuild\ch01\Buil
  dOutput\incBuild\print-info-03-v4.proj".
  Copying file from "C:\InsideMSBuild\ch01\say-hello-01.proj" to "C:\InsideMSBuild\ch01\BuildOut
  put\incBuild\say-hello-01.proj".
  Copying file from "C:\InsideMSBuild\ch01\say-hello-02.proj" to "C:\InsideMSBuild\ch01\BuildOut
  put\incBuild\say-hello-02.proj".
  Copying file from "C:\InsideMSBuild\ch01\tasks-01.proj" to "C:\InsideMSBuild\ch01\BuildOutput\
  incBuild\tasks-01.proj".
  Copying file from "C:\InsideMSBuild\ch01\tasks-02.proj" to "C:\InsideMSBuild\ch01\BuildOutput\
  incBuild\tasks-02.proj".
AfterCopyFiles:
  xxxxx AfterCopyFiles target executing
Done Building Project "C:\InsideMSBuild\ch01\inc-build-01.proj" (default targets).
```

FIGURE 1-16 The result of building Inc-build-01.proj when the BuildOutput\IncBuild folder is empty.

Because the files in the BuildOutput\IncBuild directory do not exist, all the source files will be overwritten. You can see from the result in Figure 1-16 that the AfterCopyFiles target was successfully executed as expected. Now let's see what the result is when we build Inc-build-01.proj a second time. The result is shown in Figure 1-17.

```
C:\InsideMSBuild\ch01>msbuild inc-build-01.proj /nologo
Build started 12/25/2012 9:54:32 PM.
Project "C:\InsideMSBuild\ch01\inc-build-01.proj" on node 1 (default targets).
CopyFiles:
Skipping target "CopyFiles" because all output files are up-to-date with respect to the input fi
les.
AfterCopyFiles:
  xxxxx AfterCopyFiles target executing
Done Building Project "C:\InsideMSBuild\ch01\inc-build-01.proj" (default targets).
```

FIGURE 1-17 The result of building Inc-build-01.proj again.

In the result, you can see that the CopyFile target was completely skipped, but the AfterCopyFiles target was not skipped at all. Because the AfterCopyFiles target does not have any inputs or outputs, it will never be skipped. So how can we execute AfterCopyFiles only if the CopyFiles target is executed? You might think that you could copy the inputs and outputs from CopyFiles and paste them on the AfterCopyFiles target. This doesn't work because the CopyFiles target executes before AfterCopyFiles, so all the outputs will be up to date every time AfterCopyFiles target is ready to execute. Because of that, the target will always be skipped.

In short, there is no straightforward way to ensure that the AfterCopyFiles target gets executed only when CopyFiles is. You could manage the inputs and outputs of the AfterCopyFiles target to achieve this, but there is no built-in support that we can use for the general case.

So now let's go back to the original question, which relates specifically to how Microsoft Visual Basic and C# projects are built. The target that calls the C# or Visual Basic compiler is CoreCompile, which you can find in the Microsoft.CSharp.targets file for C# and Microsoft.VisualBasic.targets file for Visual Basic. If you look at that target carefully, you might notice the following *CallTarget* invocation at the end:

```
<CallTarget Targets="$(TargetsTriggeredByCompilation)"
            Condition="'$(TargetsTriggeredByCompilation)' != ''"/>
```

In this case, *CallTarget* is being used to invoke the targets in the property *TargetsTriggeredByompilation*. In order to have your target executed when your project artifacts are built, all you need to do is to append your target to this list. You can find an example of how to accomplish this in CoreCompileExtension.csproj. The elements added to this file are shown in the following code fragment:

```
<PropertyGroup>
  <TargetsTriggeredByCompilation>
    $(TargetsTriggeredByCompilation);
    CustomAfterCompile
  </TargetsTriggeredByCompilation>
</PropertyGroup>

<Target Name="CustomAfterCompile">
  <Message Text="********* CustomAfterCompile executed"
           Importance="high"/>
</Target>
```

Here, you can see that the CustomAfterCompile target is appended to the *TargetsTriggeredByompilation* list. You append to this list instead of simply overwriting it because other targets may be using this same feature. By using this technique, if the CoreCompile target is skipped, your target will not be executed either. Now let's move on to another sample, which shows how we can inject a new target into the build process of a project.

How to extend the build process without modifying the project you are building (target injection)

There are many scenarios where you may need to extend the build process for several different projects. For example, when you are executing a Release build on your build server, you may want to run a custom tool on all your source files before the project is built. How can we extend the build process for projects when they are executed on your build server, but only for Release builds? In the previous edition, in Chapter 8, "Practical Applications, Part 1," we described how the Microsoft.Common.targets file will import known files automatically, if they exist. We already have described one way to achieve this goal, but that solution would affect every build on the build server. We want to be able to have a bit more control when the file gets imported in this scenario. Two properties can help us with that.

If you remember from Chapter 8, in Microsoft.Common.targets at the top of the file, you will find the following *Import* statement:

```
<Import Project="$(CustomBeforeMicrosoftCommonTargets)"
   Condition="'$(CustomBeforeMicrosoftCommonTargets)' != '' and
   Exists('$(CustomBeforeMicrosoftCommonTargets)')"/>
```

And similarly, at the bottom of the file, you will find the next *Import* statement:

```
<Import Project="$(CustomAfterMicrosoftCommonTargets)"
    Condition="'$(CustomAfterMicrosoftCommonTargets)' != '' and
    Exists('$(CustomAfterMicrosoftCommonTargets)')"/>
```

From the sample in Chapter 8, we simply placed the file in the default location for these files. Instead of that, we can simply specify the file path for either CustomBeforeMicrosoftCommonTargets or CustomAfterMicrosoftCommonTargets. By default, I use CustomAfterMicrosoftCommonTargets to ensure that all the properties/items of the project itself are made available to my build script. There may be some cases where you will need to use the alternate property. Now let's show how to use this technique.

In the samples, you will find Extend-build-01.proj, the contents of which are shown in the following code block:

```
<Project ToolsVersion="4.0" DefaultTargets="Demo" xmlns="http://schemas.microsoft.com/developer/
msbuild/2003">

  <ItemGroup>
    <ProjectsToBuild Include="Samples.Ch01\Samples.Ch01.csproj"/>
    <ProjectsToBuild Include="Samples.Ch01.v2\Samples.Ch01.v2.csproj"/>
    <ProjectsToBuild Include="Samples.Ch01.v4\Samples.Ch01.v4.csproj"/>
  </ItemGroup>

  <Target Name="Demo">
    <MSBuild Projects="@(ProjectsToBuild)"
             Properties="CustomAfterMicrosoftCommonTargets=
                $(MSBuildThisFileDirectory)extend-build-01-After.proj">
      <Output ItemName="ProjOutputs" TaskParameter="TargetOutputs"/>
    </MSBuild>

    <Message Text="ProjOutputs: @(ProjOutputs)"/>
  </Target>
</Project>
```

In this build script, you can see that we have defined an item called ProjectsToBuild. This contains a list of C# projects that will be built. We pass this item list to the MSBuild task so that it can be built. When we do so, we pass the additional property *CustomAfterMicrosoftCommonTargets=$(MSBuildT hisFileDirectory)extend-build-01-After.proj*. Because of this, the file Extend-build-01-After.proj will be imported automatically into the build process for each of the C# projects. Let's look at the contents of that file, shown in the next code snippet:

```
<Project ToolsVersion="4.0" xmlns="http://schemas.microsoft.com/developer/msbuild/2003">

  <Target Name="RunCustomTool" Outputs="@(Compile)">
    <Message Text="*** Running custom tool on  the following source files. ***"
             Importance="high"/>

    <Message Text="%(Compile.FullPath)"/>
  </Target>

  <PropertyGroup>
```

```
    <BuildDependsOn>
      $(BuildDependsOn);
      RunCustomTool
    </BuildDependsOn>
  </PropertyGroup>

</Project>
```

This project file is pretty simple. It contains one target declaration, as well as a PropertyGroup. The target, RunCustomTool, will run the custom tool on all the source files. In this sample, we just output the full path of the files that will be compiled. This target gets appended to the targets that will be executed by prepending it to the *BuildDependsOn* property. Let's look at the output when we execute the command `msbuild.exe extend-build-01.proj` (see Figure 1-18).

```
C:\InsideMSBuild\ch01>msbuild extend-build-01.proj /nologo
Build started 12/27/2012 4:19:38 PM.
Project "C:\InsideMSBuild\ch01\extend-build-01.proj" on node 1 (default targets).
Project "C:\InsideMSBuild\ch01\extend-build-01.proj" (1) is building "C:\InsideMSBui
ld\ch01\Samples.Ch01\Samples.Ch01.csproj" (2) on node 1 (default targets).
RunCustomTool:
  *** Running custom tool on  the following source files. ***
  C:\InsideMSBuild\ch01\Samples.Ch01\PrintInfo.cs
  C:\InsideMSBuild\ch01\Samples.Ch01\Properties\AssemblyInfo.cs
  C:\InsideMSBuild\ch01\Samples.Ch01\SayHello.cs
GenerateTargetFrameworkMonikerAttribute:
Skipping target "GenerateTargetFrameworkMonikerAttribute" because all output files a
re up-to-date with respect to the input files.
CoreCompile:
Skipping target "CoreCompile" because all output files are up-to-date with respect t
o the input files.
CopyFilesToOutputDirectory:
  Samples.Ch01 -> C:\InsideMSBuild\ch01\Samples.Ch01\bin\Debug\Samples.Ch01.dll
Done Building Project "C:\InsideMSBuild\ch01\Samples.Ch01\Samples.Ch01.csproj" (defa
ult targets).

Project "C:\InsideMSBuild\ch01\extend-build-01.proj" (1) is building "C:\InsideMSBui
ld\ch01\Samples.Ch01.v2\Samples.Ch01.v2.csproj" (3) on node 1 (default targets).
RunCustomTool:
  *** Running custom tool on  the following source files. ***
  C:\InsideMSBuild\ch01\Samples.Ch01.v2\PrintInfo.cs
  C:\InsideMSBuild\ch01\Samples.Ch01.v2\Properties\AssemblyInfo.cs
  C:\InsideMSBuild\ch01\Samples.Ch01.v2\SayHello.cs
CoreCompile:
```

FIGURE 1-18 The result when building Extend-build-01.proj.

In Figure 1-18, you can see that when each project is built, the RunCustomTool target is executed before the build process for each individual project. This is actually really fascinating, and it also can be very useful for build lab scenarios. I like to call this *target injection,* as we can literally inject targets (and other elements) into the build process for a given project without even changing it. The approach shown here is good, but it has one drawback. It requires that you create and maintain two different MSBuild files. It would be better if we could achieve the same thing with a single file. As it turns out, we can; let's see how to do that.

In the previous example, we have two different MSBuild files being used: Extend-build-01.proj, which is the file driving the build process, and Extend-build-01-after.proj, which is the file containing the elements being injected. We can basically combine both of these files. Take a look at the contents of the file Extend-build-02.proj:

```xml
<Project ToolsVersion="4.0" DefaultTargets="Demo"
         xmlns="http://schemas.microsoft.com/developer/msbuild/2003">

  <ItemGroup>
    <ProjectsToBuild Include="Samples.Ch01\Samples.Ch01.csproj"/>
    <ProjectsToBuild Include="Samples.Ch01.v2\Samples.Ch01.v2.csproj"/>
    <ProjectsToBuild Include="Samples.Ch01.v4\Samples.Ch01.v4.csproj"/>
  </ItemGroup>

  <Target Name="Demo">
    <MSBuild Projects="@(ProjectsToBuild)"
             Properties="CustomAfterMicrosoftCommonTargets=$(MSBuildThisFileFullPath)">
      <Output ItemName="ProjOutputs" TaskParameter="TargetOutputs"/>
    </MSBuild>

    <Message Text="ProjOutputs: @(ProjOutputs)"/>
  </Target>


  <!-- This section is the portion which is required to be imported -->
  <Target Name="RunCustomTool" Outputs="@(Compile)">
    <Message Text="*** Running custom tool on  the following source files. ***"
             Importance="high"/>

    <Message Text="%(Compile.FullPath)"/>
  </Target>

  <PropertyGroup>
    <BuildDependsOn>
      RunCustomTool;
      $(BuildDependsOn);
    </BuildDependsOn>
  </PropertyGroup>

</Project>
```

This project file contains all the elements from both files, and the invocation of the MSBuild target has been updated to pass in `CustomAfterMicrosoftCommonTargets=$(MSBuildThisFileFull Path)`". If you build this file, you will see that the result is the same as building the Extend-build-01. proj file. The drawback of having everything in a single file is that when your target projects get built, you will be importing elements that may be irrelevant to that build process. For example, the Demo target is imported for each C# project being built, and it is not always needed. In many cases, this will not be an issue, but if there is a property/item name collision, that could cause some conflicts.

In this chapter, we have covered what's new with MSBuild 4.5 as well as updates to related technologies. There may not have been a lot of core updates to the MSBuild engine, but there have been significant updates to how projects are built. For example, when Visual Studio 2010 was released, NuGet and Project Compatibility were not available with older Visual Studio versions. Both of these items have a significant impact on the build process for Visual Studio solutions. Now that we have covered what's new in and around MSBuild, let's move on to look at the Team Build updates.

CHAPTER 2

What's new in Team Foundation Build 2012

I n the first part of this chapter, we'll look at the new features that are available in Team Foundation Build 2012, as well as the improvements to Microsoft Windows Workflow Foundation 4.5 that you can use when customizing or creating build process templates. In the second part of this chapter, we'll look at how to use some of these new features, step by step.

Installation

The installation process for Team Foundation Build 2012 is largely unchanged from Team Foundation Build 2010, but there have been some changes to system requirements as well as improved support for unattended installation, which we'll cover in this section.

System requirements

The system requirements for Team Foundation Build 2012 have not changed significantly. The hardware requirements are the same, but Team Foundation Build 2012 now supports the following operating systems:

- 64-bit version of Windows Server 2008 with SP2 (Standard or Enterprise edition)

- 64-bit version of Windows Server 2008 R2 with SP1 (Standard or Enterprise edition)

- 64-bit version of Windows Server 2012

- 32- and 64-bit versions of Windows 7 with SP1 (Home Premium, Professional, Enterprise, or Ultimate edition)

- 32- and 64-bit versions of Windows 8

This means that Team Foundation Build 2012 is not supported on Windows XP, Windows Vista, Windows Server 2003, or 32-bit versions of Windows Server 2008.

Unattended installation

Team Foundation Build 2012 also supports unattended installation by allowing configuration to be done unattended using the Tfsconfig command-line tool. There are three steps to performing an unattended installation of Team Foundation Build 2012:

1. Create an unattended configuration file. A stub configuration file can be created by running tfsconfig unattend /create /type:build /unattendfile:unattend.ini.

2. Perform an unattended installation by running `tfs_server.exe /quiet` from the installation media. Because installing Microsoft .NET Framework 4.5 requires a reboot if it's not already installed, it may be necessary to run this command, reboot, and then run it again before Team Foundation Build 2012 is fully installed.

3. Perform an unattended configuration by running `tfsconfig unattend /configure / unattendfile:unattend.ini` using the Unattend.ini file created in step 1.

> **Tip** The Tfsconfig.exe file is located in %ProgramFiles%\Microsoft Team Foundation Server 11.0\Tools once Team Foundation Build 2012 has been installed.

In the "Team Foundation Build 2012 cookbook" section later in this chapter, we'll look at how to implement a common unattended installation scenario in more depth.

Team Foundation Service

Perhaps the biggest change in Team Foundation Build 2012 is one that isn't technically part of Microsoft Visual Studio 2012 or Team Foundation Server 2012—the introduction of Team Foundation Service.

The Team Foundation Service is a cloud-based version of Team Foundation Server, which allows you to use Team Foundation Server in a matter of minutes, without having to set up your own infrastructure. A Free Plan is available, which supports up to five users with an unlimited number of team projects. It also supports a wide variety of the features available in the on-premise Team Foundation Server, including the following:

- Version control (including Git support)

- Work item tracking

- Agile planning tools

- Build (currently in "preview")

- Test management (currently in "preview")

Currently, the Build service is in "preview," which means it can be used without charge. According to the service's pricing page, when the feature exits this "preview" mode, a certain number of builds will be available for free each month (if you're on the Free Plan), and builds beyond that will incur an additional charge.

The Team Foundation Service supports both on-premise build controllers and agents (where they're hosted on your hardware and network) and a single build controller/agent (per account) hosted in the cloud. To use the hosted build controller/agent, simply select Hosted Build Controller from the Build Defaults tab of the New Build Definition dialog box, as shown in Figure 2-1.

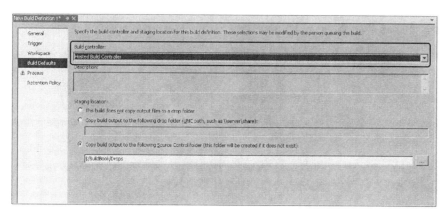

FIGURE 2-1 Selecting the Hosted Build Controller.

On this tab, you may also notice a new option for the drop location (now called Staging Location) that allows you to put the build outputs into version control. This option is available only for build definitions on the Team Foundation Service and is very important because the Team Foundation Service does not have access to a Universal Naming Convention (UNC) path to drop the build outputs. This path needs to be placed under the drop's folder at the root of each team project, and a subdirectory will be created automatically under the selected path based on the build definition's name. If you choose to delete drops as part of your retention policy, the drop's folder in version control will be destroyed so that that space can be reclaimed by the database.

Each time you build using the Hosted Build Controller, you'll notice a short delay before the build begins. This delay is because the build controller/agent is reimaged automatically before each build.

The Hosted Build Controller is a single machine per each account, so it will be shared across all the team projects and build definitions in that account. It is the quickest and easiest way to start using builds in the Team Foundation Service, but it does have a number of limitations that may affect its suitability for your purposes. This machine will run only a single build at a time, which may be a problem if you have a large number of build definitions or need to process a large number of builds.

If you determine that the Hosted Build Controller won't meet your needs, then you can use on-premise build controllers/agents, which is discussed in the "Team Foundation Build 2012 cookbook" section of this chapter. Some of the limitations of the Hosted Build Controller are

- The build process does not run with administrative privileges on the build controller/agent.

- The build controller/agent may not have the software installed that your build process requires. A list of the software installed on the build controller/agent is available at *http://tfs.visualstudio.com/en-us/learn/build/hosted-build-controller-in-vs/#software.*

- The most significant limitation is that the Hosted Build Controller cannot build Windows Store applications.

- Because the build process does not run with administrative privileges, you can't install software as part of the build process template to work around this limitation. However, you can use software that can be XCopy-deployed (including *NuGet* packages).

- The build controller/agent has 1 GB of free space for source code, intermediate outputs, and build outputs.

- The build process is limited to a maximum execution time of 1 hour.

- The build controller/agent does not run interactively, so it cannot run tests that require an interactive session (such as Coded UI tests).

- You do not have the capability to log on to the build controller/agent machine, which may affect your ability to debug custom build process templates.

You can still customize build process templates in the Team Foundation Service, just as you can for Team Foundation Server. However, you need to keep these limitations in mind to ensure that your customizations work in the hosted environment. You can detect programmatically whether you're running in the Team Foundation Service by using the *IsVirtual* property of *IBuildServiceHost*, which is accessible using the *ServiceHost* property from either *IBuildController* or *IBuildAgent*.

User interface (UI) enhancements

This section covers the user interface (UI) enhancements that are in Visual Studio 2012 and Team Foundation Server 2012 Web Access, including the significant update to Team Explorer.

Team Explorer

Visual Studio 2012 includes a significant update of the Team Explorer user interface, which is now streamlined to make common tasks easier to complete and to provide "at-a-glance" information within Team Explorer itself. The hierarchical tree that had been in previous versions is now replaced with a series of pages that focus on specific tasks. Figure 2-2 shows the Builds page of Team Explorer, which replaces the Builds tree node from Visual Studio 2010.

FIGURE 2-2 Builds page of Team Explorer.

My Builds

The My Builds section (see Figure 2-3) automatically shows your six most recent builds, which allows you to see at a glance the outcome of recent builds that you've triggered. Double-clicking a build takes you to that build's details, and right-clicking it allows you to take actions quickly, such as retaining a build, retrying a failed build, or reconciling your workspace after a gated check-in. You can also click Actions and My Builds to open Build Explorer in a form that is filtered based on builds you queued.

FIGURE 2-3 My Builds section in Team Explorer.

All Build Definitions

The All Build Definitions section provides a number of improvements from the Builds tree view that was available in Visual Studio 2010.

Teams with a large number of build definitions will appreciate that Build Explorer now has the ability to filter the list of build definitions, as shown in Figure 2-4. As you type in the Search box (signified by the magnifying glass icon), the list of build definitions will be filtered to ones whose names contain the search text.

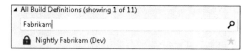

FIGURE 2-4 Build definition search.

Each build definition now has an icon that provides two pieces of information about it: what type of trigger it uses, and an overlay that indicates whether it is paused or disabled. Figure 2-5 shows a build definition of each trigger type, along with its associated icon and information on its status (Batched, Paused, Disabled, and so on).

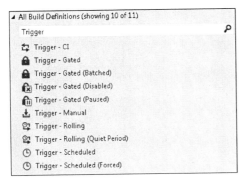

FIGURE 2-5 Trigger icons for build definitions.

One feature that at first appears to be missing from Visual Studio 2012 is the ability to double-click All Definitions to view the whole build queue. However, you can still get to this view by clicking Actions and then Manage Queue.

Favorites

You can mark a build definition as a favorite by right-clicking it in Team Explorer and choosing Add To Favorites. You'll then see the build definition listed in the My Favorite Build Definitions section, as shown in Figure 2-6, with a summary of the most recent build that completed and a histogram showing the last nine builds for that build definition. Pausing over the definition will give you a summary of the definition, including what trigger it uses, whether it's enabled or not, and information about the most recent build. It is also possible to make a build definition a Team Favorite, but this can be done only from Web Access.

Extensibility

Visual Studio 2012 supports extending Team Explorer by adding new pages and adding sections to existing pages. In the "Team Foundation Build 2012 cookbook" section of this chapter, we'll show you an example of extending the Builds page with new functionality.

Queue details

In Visual Studio 2010, you couldn't double-click a queued build to view details about it; but in Visual Studio 2012, when you double-click a queued build (technically a build request), you see the Build Request window, shown in Figure 2-7. This window provides information about how many requests are queued for the build controller, as well as the build definition that this build request is for, the position of this specific request in the queue, and the average wait time in the queue and build time based on previous builds. In addition, the Build Request window warns you if the build definition has been paused.

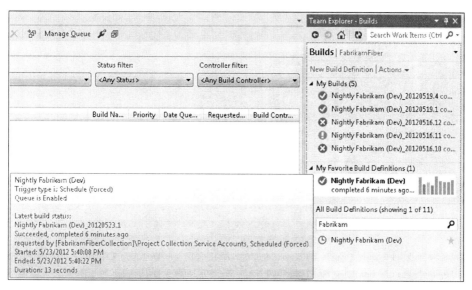

FIGURE 2-6 Favorite build definitions in Team Explorer.

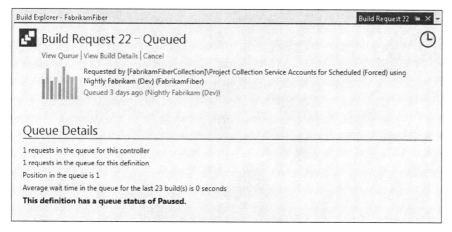

FIGURE 2-7 Queue details in the Build Request window.

Web Access

One of the side effects of the introduction of the Team Foundation Service is that web access in Team Foundation Server 2012 has become more feature-rich. The home page for a team (see Figure 2-8) shows a tile for each build definition that has been marked as a Team Favorite. This tile shows the same histogram that is shown in Team Explorer, and although pausing over the bars of the histogram will show you information about each of the builds, clicking an individual bar won't take you to that build's details as it does in Team Explorer. Rather, clicking anywhere inside the time will take you to Build Explorer and show you recently completed builds for that build definition.

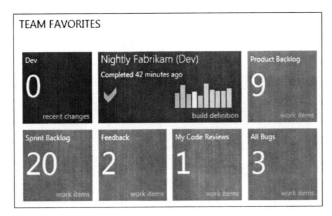

FIGURE 2-8 Team Favorites in Web Access.

Now you can also queue builds from within Web Access by clicking the Queue Build link on the Build Explorer page. You can specify basic settings when queuing the build, as shown in Figure 2-9, but you can't specify values for any custom parameters, which may limit the usefulness of this feature.

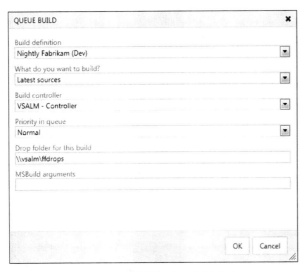

FIGURE 2-9 The Queue Build dialog box in Web Access.

Visual Studio Test Runner

Visual Studio 2010 was limited to running MSTest-based unit tests, but Visual Studio 2012 now supports third-party unit testing frameworks, and this support extends to Team Build 2012. Individual unit testing frameworks may have their own installation and configuration steps, but at a high level, the process for using a third-party unit testing framework is as follows:

1. Install the unit test framework's Visual Studio extension on the developer's machines to install the necessary test assemblies and provide integration with Test Explorer.

2. Check the unit test framework's assemblies into your build controller's custom assemblies location to allow the tests to be run automatically as part of the build.

3. Modify the build definition to use the Visual Studio Test Runner, as shown in Figure 2-10. To get to this dialog box, click the Process tab in the build definition, click the Automated Tests parameter in the Basic category, and then click the ellipsis button that appears.

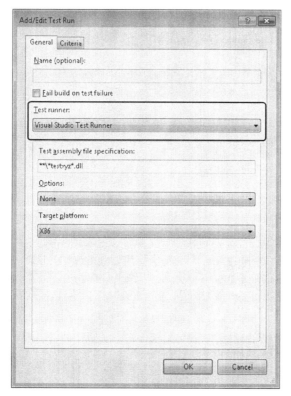

FIGURE 2-10 Selecting the Visual Studio Test Runner.

Note When upgrading from Team Foundation Server 2010 to Team Foundation Server 2012, the build definitions will default to using the MSTest.exe Test Runner or the MSTest Test Metadata File Test Runner, each of which provides backward compatibility with Team Foundation Server 2010.

Pausing build definitions

In Team Build 2010, build definitions could have only two statuses: enabled or disabled. Team Build 2012 introduces a new Paused status for build definitions, as shown in Figure 2-11.

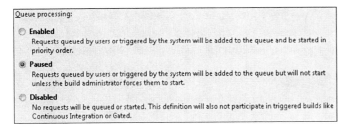

FIGURE 2-11 Paused queue status.

When a build definition is disabled, manual builds can't be queued; scheduled, rolling, and continuous integration builds won't be queued; and check-ins that normally would be gated by the definition will be checked in directly.

When a definition is paused, builds will be queued as if the definition is enabled, but they won't be processed until either the build definition is enabled or the build is forced to start by an administrator. Builds can be forced to start by right-clicking the paused build in Build Explorer and choosing Start Now.

Being able to pause definitions can be valuable when you have a high throughput of check-ins and need to make potentially destabilizing changes to the branch. For example, here's how you could use the Pause Definition feature to take an integration into a branch while minimizing the disruption to other developers that are submitting changes:

1. Pause the build definition that covers the branch.

2. Perform the integration and submit it to gated check-in. It will be queued but not processed, like any other check-in.

3. Right-click the build for the integration and choose Start Now.

4. If the build succeeds, enable the build definition, which will allow the other queued builds to be processed.

5. If the build doesn't succeed, submit check-ins to fix the issues and force them through using Start Now. Once all the issues have been resolved, unpause the build definition.

Batching

For teams with a high volume of check-ins or long running builds, adopting gated check-in can result in throughput that doesn't keep up with demand. Team Build 2012 introduces the concept of batching, which will group multiple gated check-ins into a single build in an attempt to build them together. If this succeeds, all the changesets will be checked in; otherwise, the check-ins will be retried individually as separate builds.

Batching is enabled by checking the Merge And Build Up To X Submissions check box on the build definition's Trigger tab (see Figure 2-12) and entering the maximum number of submissions that can be in each batch.

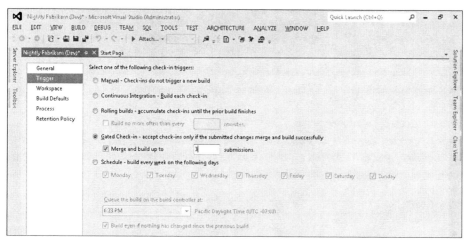

FIGURE 2-12 Enabling batching when editing a build definition.

> **Tip** Batching too many builds together can increase the chance of merge conflicts and build and test failures, which can result in decreased throughput. Therefore, you need to experiment to determine the optimal batch size for your build definitions.

Batching is based on a new concept in Team Build 2012 called *requests*. Anytime a build is needed, it starts as a request. If the trigger does not support batching, then each request will trigger a single build. However, if the trigger does support batching, then a build may include multiple requests. Figure 2-13 displays a batched gated check-in build that includes two requests.

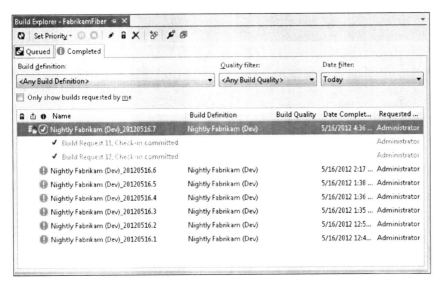

FIGURE 2-13 Build Explorer showing a successful build containing two requests.

If the build succeeds, then these requests have now been completed. However, if the build fails, those requests can be pushed back into the queue and trigger additional builds. This means that a build can include multiple requests, but also that a request may be part of multiple builds. In Figure 2-14, you can see a request that is included as part of multiple builds.

FIGURE 2-14 Build Explorer showing a failed build containing two requests.

In Figure 2-14, you can also see a second batching behavior. The build 20120516.8 contains two requests: one that contained a change that would compile successfully (Build Request 13) and one that wouldn't (Build Request 14). This build failed because of a compilation error, but the

DefaultProcessTemplate then queued the requests to be retried individually. The retries subsequently became builds 20120516.9 (which contained Build Request 13) and 20120516.10 (which contained Build Request 14). Because Build Request 13 compiled successfully by itself, it was committed; but Build Request 14 still failed to compile, so it was rejected (and not retried again).

You can also determine what requests make up a build and what builds a request was part of using the Team Build application programming interface (API). The IBuildDetail interface has a new property called *Requests,* which returns a read-only collection of *IQueuedBuild* instances that initiated the build. You can also determine the builds that a request was a part of during its lifetime using the *Builds* property on *IQueuedBuild.*

This default behavior provides the best of both worlds because changes that batch together successfully will provide high throughput. When the batch fails to build successfully, though, the individual requests will be built individually, providing additional feedback about the cause of the failure and allowing valid requests to still be committed. This behavior exists during the sync, build, and test phases of the build process, although during sync, because it's possible to determine the specific requests that caused the failure, only the requests that failed to unshelve will be retried, and the rest will continue to build.

Besides batching, there are other ways in which a request may be associated with multiple builds. If you retry a build (as described in the "User interface (UI) enhancements" section earlier in this chapter), the requests in that build will be associated with the new build. If a build controller loses connectivity with the Team Foundation Server, any builds that it runs will be retried automatically, causing the requests in those builds to be associated with multiple builds.

The logic that accepts, rejects, or retries requests is driven by activities called from the workflow, which enables you to add batching support to your custom build process templates or modify the default batching logic in the out-of-the-box template.

Logging

Team Build 2012 introduces two new features to help debug build and infrastructure issues. The first, diagnostic logging, makes diagnostic logs available regardless of the logging verbosity shown in the build log; and the second is Operational and Analytic logs on the build controllers and agents themselves.

Diagnostic logging

Diagnostic logging is one of the most useful tools when debugging build process template issues because it includes the inputs and outputs for each activity, as well as including activities that have been configured to log only at higher verbosity levels. In Team Build 2010, you enabled diagnostic logging by setting the Logging Verbosity option to Diagnostic in the build definition, or when queuing the build, which would increase the verbosity shown in Visual Studio when opening the build.

In previous versions of Team Build, it wasn't practical to leave diagnostic logging on because it made the build log harder to read, decreased the performance of viewing it, and increased the size of the TFS database unnecessarily. This meant that diagnostic logs were usually turned off, and as a result, they were rarely available when you needed them, so you would have to enable them temporarily, try to reproduce the issue (which may be time consuming or impossible), and then disable them again.

In Team Build 2012, diagnostic logs are copied to the build's drop location in XML format regardless of the logging verbosity configured in the build definition or at queue time. Because these logs are always there, it is significantly easier to investigate intermittent issues, and because they're not stored in the TFS database, they don't have an impact on the size of the database or the performance of viewing the build log in Visual Studio.

These diagnostic logs are dropped automatically by the build controller and agents when either the build completes (for the build controller) or the AgentScope exits (for the build agents). These logs are dropped to the Logs subdirectory, and you'll find a separate XML log file for the build controller and for each build agent involved in the build, as well as an Extensible Stylesheet Language (XSL) transform that will format the XML files for viewing. (See Figure 2-15 for an example of this.) To view the formatted XML files, simply open them with Windows Internet Explorer, and the XSL transformation will be applied automatically, as shown in Figure 2-16.

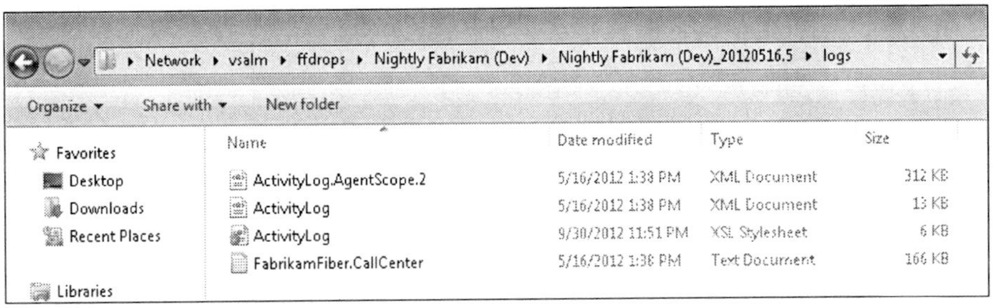

FIGURE 2-15 Diagnostic log XML files and stylesheet dropped for a build.

For long-running builds, you may want to access the diagnostic logs while the build is still running. You can do this by selecting Diagnostics and then Request Logs from the build log, as shown in Figure 2-17. When you do this, the intermediate logs will be copied to a Logs\Intermediate\<Timestamp> directory within the build's drop location. You can select Diagnostics and then View Logs to view the most recent intermediate diagnostic logs, or you can select the specific set of intermediate logs you'd like to view if you've requested them multiple times during the build. On the build controller and build agent, these logs are temporarily written to %Temp%\<BuildController|BuildAgent>\<BuildControllerId|BuildAgentId>\Logs\<BuildId>.

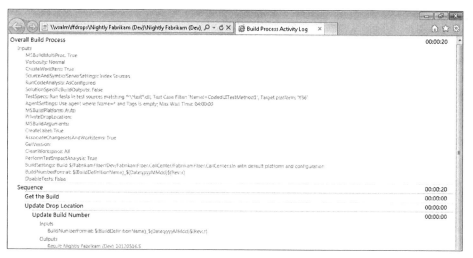

FIGURE 2-16 ActivityLog.xml opened in Internet Explorer, showing the stylesheet applied automatically.

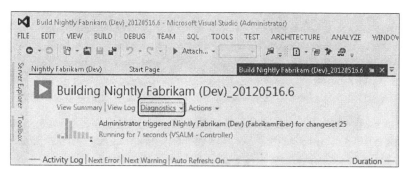

FIGURE 2-17 Requesting intermediate diagnostic logs.

Because the diagnostic logs are copied to the drop, they'll be available only if the build definition specifies a drop location on the Build Defaults tab (this is also required to request intermediate logs). If you're creating a custom build process template, then you also need to call the SetBuildProperties activity to set the drop location for the build.

Operational and Analytic logs

While diagnostic logs are useful for diagnosing build failures caused by the way the build definition is configured or by customizations that have been made to the build process template, they're of limited use in diagnosing infrastructure and connectivity issues. This is where the Operational and Analytic logs are useful.

The Operational log is low volume; it includes only events critical to the service's lifetime, such as starting the service, losing connectivity (and its subsequent return), and stopping the service. This log is enabled by default and is accessed in Event Viewer by selecting Applications And Services Logs, Microsoft, Team Foundation Server, Build-Services, and Operational, as shown in Figure 2-18.

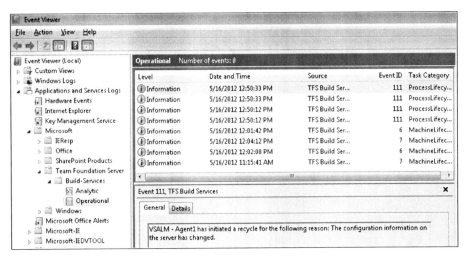

FIGURE 2-18 The Operational log in Event Viewer.

The Analytic log is very detailed; it includes all events in the service's lifetime, as well as events in each build's lifetime, such as agent reservations, workflow execution, and communications. This log is disabled by default and is accessed in Event Viewer by selecting Applications And Services Logs, Microsoft, Team Foundation Server, Build-Services, and Analytic. Event Viewer hides debug and analytic logs by default, so to view this log, you'll need to select Show Analytic And Debug Logs from the View menu in Event Viewer. To enable the log, right-click it in Event Viewer and choose Enable Log.

The Analytic log is limited to 20 MB by default and, unlike other event logs, newer events will be discarded when the size limit is reached. You can change this behavior by right-clicking the log, choosing Properties, and then choosing Overwrite Events As Needed. However, if you do this, you'll no longer be able to view the log. To view the events that have been logged, you need to disable the log first.

Analytic and debug logs are more difficult to navigate in Event Viewer than other log files because you can only page forward through them. To make the Analytic log easier to work with, you can export it to a file by right-clicking the log and choosing Save All Events As.

Windows Workflow Foundation 4.5

Team Build 2012 is based on Windows Workflow Foundation 4.5 (rather than Windows Workflow Foundation 4.0, which was used in Team Build 2010). This means that this release also includes a number of improvements to the Workflow Designer and Workflow Runtime. In this section, we'll cover some of the improvements that affect Team Build 2012.

 More Info For a more comprehensive list of Windows Workflow Foundation 4.5 changes, visit *http://msdn.microsoft.com/en-us/library/hh305677(v=VS.110).aspx*.

Workflow Designer

This release brings a number of features to the Workflow Designer that drastically improve the productivity of working with the build process templates in Team Build.

Quick Find and Find In Files

Visual Studio 2010 didn't support finding content in workflow files particularly well, which made working with large workflows or projects with a large number of custom activities difficult. In Visual Studio 2012, this functionality is now supported by Quick Find and Find In Files.

The first improvement is Quick Find, which is invoked by pressing Ctrl+F from within the Workflow Designer. When doing a search in the current document, it will match workflow arguments and variables, as well as activity properties and arguments (including their display names). In Figure 2-19, you can see the result of doing a Quick Find in a build process template (especially the tooltip, which describes where the match was found).

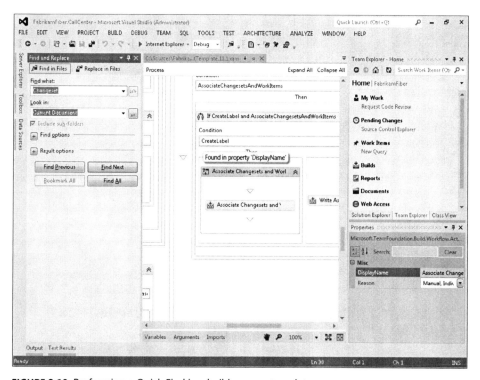

FIGURE 2-19 Performing a Quick Find in a build process template.

Visual Studio 2012 also includes improvements to Find In Files. When you double-click a search result, it will open the associated Extensible Application Markup Language (XAML) file and automatically navigate to the location of the search result within that workflow.

Outline view

Navigating around a large workflow in Visual Studio 2010, you either needed to expand the entire workflow and browse it that way, or search for the correct hierarchy to expand to find what you want. In either case, you were slowed down by the Workflow Designer repainting as you navigated around the interface. While the find improvements help somewhat, that's only if you know what you're looking for.

Visual Studio 2012 now supports the document outline view (which was available previously for other hierarchical files such as HTML) for workflow files. You can open this view by clicking View, Other Windows, and Document Outline. In Figure 2-20, you can see the document outline for the DefaultProcessTemplate build process template. Note that when you click an activity in the document outline, it will take the Workflow Designer to the location of that activity and select it.

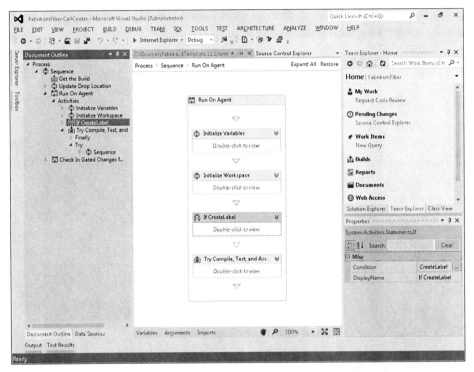

FIGURE 2-20 The document outline view of the DefaultProcessTemplate build process template.

Auto-Surround with Sequence

Most activities which have children (such as *If, While,* and *Parallel*) only support a single child activity. This isn't as much of a limitation as it seems because that single child activity can be a Sequence, which can contain multiple children. However, it can make using the Workflow Designer in Visual Studio 2010 frustrating.

For example, if you had an *If* activity that you only wanted to execute for a single activity, you'd just drag that activity in. But if you decided later that you wanted to add a second activity, you'd need to remove that activity, replace it with a sequence, add the original activity back in, and then add your new activity.

The Workflow Designer in Visual Studio 2012 includes a new feature called Auto-Surround With Sequence. With this feature, if you drag an activity to a location that supports only a single activity and there's already an activity in that location, the Workflow Designer will surround them both with a new Sequence activity automatically.

Annotations

Clear and concise comments that describe intent improve the understandability of code and, because workflows are essentially graphical code, they'd benefit just as much from containing comments. In Visual Studio 2010, there were a couple of workarounds that allowed you to do this: either adding XML comments to the XAML itself (which wouldn't be visible in the Workflow Designer), or adding such comments as the DisplayName to activities that don't have any behavior, such as sequences (which adds noise to the workflow's structure). Both of these approaches have their drawbacks.

Windows Workflow Foundation 4.5 adds a first-class commenting feature called *annotations*. You can add an annotation to any activity by right-clicking it, clicking Annotations, and then clicking Add Annotation. Figure 2-21 shows an activity which has had an annotation applied to it.

FIGURE 2-21 Workflow activity with an annotation applied.

Workflow Runtime

Because Team Build is its own workflow host, the majority of improvements to the Workflow Runtime don't apply to the Team Build environment. There is one improvement worth discussing, however, and that is support for C# expressions.

C# Expressions

One of the most anticipated features of Windows Workflow Foundation 4.5 is support for C# expressions. Unfortunately, Team Build 2012 does not fully support this feature. The build process templates themselves are still restricted to using Microsoft Visual Basic expressions because they do not get compiled. If you try to deploy a build process template that uses C# expressions, you'll see a *NotSupportedException*.

Custom activity libraries, which get deployed as a compiled assembly, can fully use C# expressions and can be consumed by the build process template without any problems. Note that you can't mix and match activities that use different expression languages in the same assembly, so if you have existing assemblies in your custom activities, you'll either need to fully convert the existing activities to use C# expressions or put your C# activities in a separate assembly.

Team Foundation Build 2012 cookbook

In this section, we'll provide step-by-step instructions on how to implement and customize some of the new features in Team Foundation Build 2012, as well as address common questions and problems that people have encountered when using Team Foundation Build.

Unattended installation and configuration

The most common unattended installation scenario is providing a new build agent and adding it to an existing build controller, so that's the situation we're going to show you. To perform these steps, you'll need a machine that already has a Team Foundation Server 2012 installation on it, which can be either the server itself or an existing build controller or agent.

The first task is to generate a configuration file for the unattended installation, which is done by performing the following steps:

1. Open a command prompt in %ProgramFiles%\Microsoft Team Foundation Server 11.0\Tools.

2. Run `tfsconfig.exe unattend /create /type:build /unattendfile:"%Temp%\Unattendbuild.xml"` to create a stub configuration file. You can replace *%Temp%\Unattendbuild.xml* with the location and file name of your choice.

3. Edit %Temp%\Unattendbuild.xml (or whatever file you are working with) using the text editor of your choice. The stub configuration file assumes that you're setting up a new controller and agents, so you'll need to make a few changes to implement this scenario.

4. Change ConfigurationType from **create** to **scale,** which causes agents to be added to an existing controller rather than creating a new one.

5. Verify that the AgentCount setting is the number of agents you want created on each machine that you perform the unattended installation on.

6. Rename the NewControllerName setting to **ExistingControllerName** and change its value to the name of the controller you want the agents to be added to. This is the name of the controller as it's shown in the Manage Build Controllers dialog box in Figure 2-22, not the machine name.

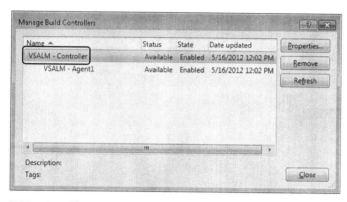

FIGURE 2-22 The Manage Build Controllers dialog box showing the controller name.

7. Verify that the CollectionUrl setting is correct. If you generated the stub configuration file from a machine that is already connected to the correct Team Project Collection, then this should already be correct.

8. Specify the credentials that the Team Build service will run with in the ServiceAccountName and ServiceAccountPassword settings. Depending on how your Team Foundation Server is configured, you can either use a built-in account (for example, NT AUTHORITY\NETWORK SERVICE) or a domain account.

9. Save the file and copy it to a location that is available from the build machines you want to configure. In this example, we'll assume that the file was copied to the same location (%Temp%\Unattendbuild.xml, or the file name you chose to work with) on the machine being configured. The resulting file for this example is

```
[Configuration]
Activity=Microsoft.TeamFoundation.Admin.TeamBuildActivity

Assembly=Microsoft.TeamFoundation.Admin, Version=11.0.0.0, Culture=neutral,
PublicKeyToken=b03f5f7f11d50a3a

; You can submit information about your Team Foundation Server configuration and administration
experience to Microsoft.
SendFeedback=True
```

```
; The type of build configuration to perform.  'Create' creates and agent and controller,
'Scale' adds agents to new or existing controller, 'Replace' replaces a host, controller and/or
agents, and 'HostOnly' just creates a service host
ConfigurationType=scale

; The number of build agents to configure
AgentCount=2

; The name of the new build controller.  This is typically the machine name that the controller
runs on.
ExistingControllerName=VSALM - Controller

; Determines whether to clean up old build controllers and agents when configuring new ones
CleanResources=False

; The collection Url the build service will be configured for.
CollectionUrl=http://vsalm:8080/tfs/fabrikamfibercollection

; Boolean to determine whether the account is a built-in account
IsServiceAccountBuiltIn=False

; Account that the build Windows service will run as.  On a domain joined machine, this can be
a domain account or NT Authority\Network Service.  On a workgroup machine, it can be a local
account or NT Authority\Local Service
ServiceAccountName=VSALM\BuildSvc
ServiceAccountPassword=P2ssw0rd

; Port that the TFS web site binds to. The port must be an integer greater than 0 and less than
65535
Port=9191

; The maximum number of concurrent builds that the controller will create.
MaxConcurrentBuilds=0
```

Next, perform the unattended installation to put the Team Foundation Server 2012 binaries on the build machine by running `tfs_server.exe /quiet` from the installation media. As mentioned earlier in the chapter, if the machine doesn't already have .NET Framework 4.5 on it the first time you run this command, it will install only the prerequisites (including .NET Framework 4.5) and then exit. You then need to reboot the machine and rerun this command to install the Team Foundation Server 2012 binaries.

At this point, the Team Foundation Server 2012 binaries are on the machine, but it hasn't been configured as a build agent. That is where the unattended configuration file that we created earlier comes in. To configure the machine as a build agent, run this code:

```
"%ProgramFiles%\Microsoft Team Foundation Server 11.0\Tools\tfsconfig.exe" unattend /configure /
unattendfile:"%temp%\unattendfile.xml"
```

If you'd like to verify the configuration before applying it, you can run the following command, but this needs to be done on a machine that hasn't already been configured:

```
"%ProgramFiles%\Microsoft Team Foundation Server 11.0\Tools\tfsconfig.exe" unattend /configure /
unattendfile:"%temp%\unattendfile.xml" /verify
```

Connect on-premise build machines to the Team Foundation Service

While the easiest way to get up and running with builds on the Team Foundation Service is to use the hosted build controller/agent (and it's also the easiest one to maintain), there are some limitations to this configuration, which we discussed earlier in this chapter. If those limitations don't apply to your requirements, then rest assured that you can use on-premise build machines with the Team Foundation Service. In this section, we'll describe how to configure this.

1. On the build machine, install the Team Foundation Server 2012 binaries by running Tfs_server.exe from the installation media and following the installation steps.

2. After the installation completes, the Team Foundation Server Configuration Center (shown here) opens. Select Configure Team Foundation Build Service and click Start Wizard to configure the machine as a build controller and/or agent.

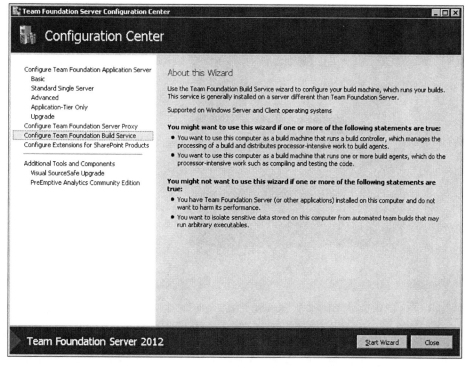

3. Click Next on the Welcome To The Build Service Configuration Wizard page.

4. On the Select A Team Project Collection page, click Browse. In the Connect To Team Project Collection dialog box, click Servers, and then click Add.

5. In the Add Team Foundation Server dialog box, shown here, enter the URL of your Team Foundation Service account and click OK.

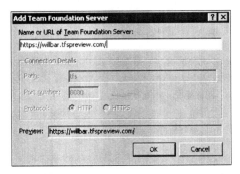

6. You'll now be prompted to authenticate your Team Foundation Service account, as shown here. The credentials that you enter will be used by Team Build whenever it needs to authenticate.

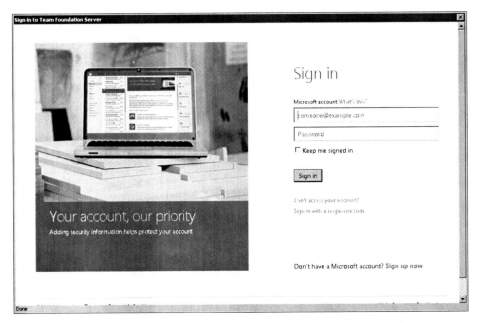

7. Click Close from the Add/Remove Team Foundation Server dialog box and then select the Team Project Collection you want to connect Team Build to. Click Connect, and then click Next.

8. If you'd like to configure this build machine as a build controller or a build controller and some number of build agents, then, on the Build Services page (shown here), choose the Use The Default Setting option and then select the number of build agents you'd like to run on the build machine (if you want the build machine to be just a build controller, select 0). For other scenarios (such as adding build agents to an existing build controller), select Configure Later. Click Next to continue.

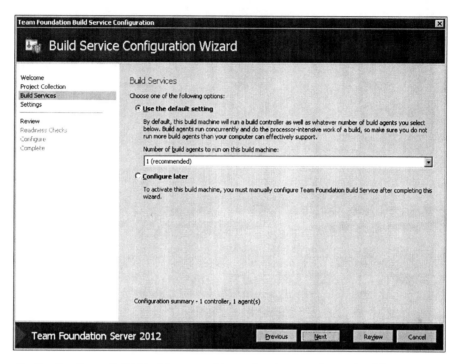

9. On the Configure Build Machine page (shown here), enter the credentials you want to run the Team Build service as. Unlike when configuring Team Build for an on-premise Team Foundation Server, these credentials won't be used to connect to the Team Foundation Service. However, because the service runs under these credentials, they will affect access to local or network resources (such as the drop location) and, depending on the corporate network configuration, may also affect the service's ability to connect to the Internet (and therefore the Team Foundation Service). Click Next to continue.

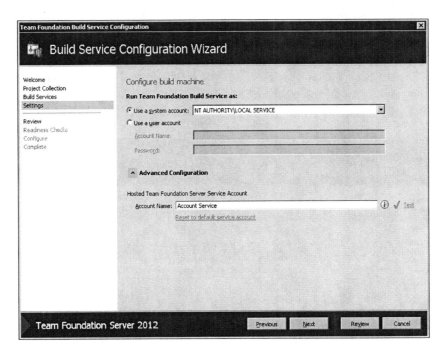

10. Review the configuration and click Next.

11. The wizard will now run the readiness checks, as shown here. If there are issues, you need to resolve them before you can complete the configuration.

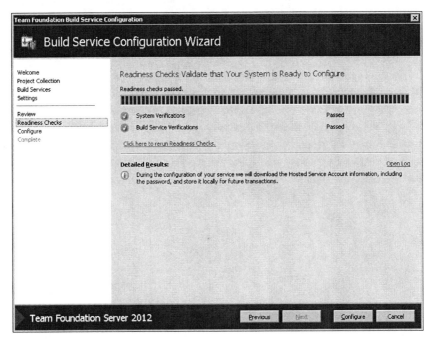

12. Finally, click Configure, and the configuration settings will be applied.

Extending Team Explorer

In this example, we're going to demonstrate adding a section to the existing Builds page of Team Explorer that shows some basic Team Build statistics.

> **More Info** For a broader overview of extending Team Explorer in Visual Studio 2012, visit Chad Boles's sample on the Visual Studio Developer Center at *http://code.msdn.microsoft* *.com/vstudio/Extending-Explorer-in-9dccd594*.

To extend Team Explorer, you first need to install the Visual Studio 2012 software development kit (SDK), which can be downloaded from *http://www.microsoft.com/en-us/download/details* *.aspx?id=30668*. Once this is done, you can proceed.

Start by creating a new project using the Visual Studio Package template in the Extensibility category of the language of your choice, as shown in Figure 2-23 (this example uses Microsoft Visual C#).

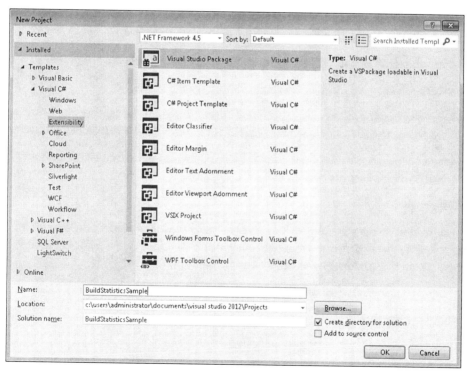

FIGURE 2-23 The New Project dialog box for a Visual Studio Package.

This will start the Visual Studio Package Wizard. For this example, you can accept the defaults on each page of the wizard, although in a real-life scenario, you should enter information to identify your package on the Basic VSPackage Information page of the wizard (shown in Figure 2-24).

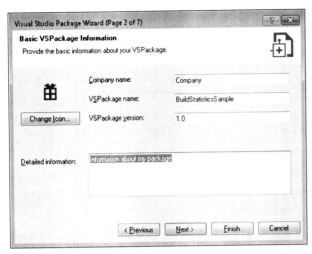

FIGURE 2-24 The Basic VSPackage Information page of the Visual Studio Package Wizard.

In the generated package project, add references to version 11.0.0.0 of the following assemblies:

- Microsoft.TeamFoundation.Build.Client (contains the Team Build API)

- Microsoft.TeamFoundation.Client (contains the core Team Foundation Server API)

- Microsoft.TeamFoundation.Controls (contains the Team Explorer API)

- Microsoft.VisualStudio.TeamFoundation.Build from %ProgramFiles%\Microsoft Visual Studio 11.0\Common7\IDE\PrivateAssemblies (contains the Team Build Visual Studio integration API)

- System.ComponentModel.Composition (contains the Managed Extensibility Framework, which is used to discover extensions)

- System.Xaml

The first thing to do once the project is created is modify the Visual Studio Extension (VSIX) manifest to specify that this project should be installed as a Managed Extensibility Framework component. To do this, perform the following steps:

1. Double-click source.extension.vsixmanifest in Solution Explorer.

2. Click the Assets tab.

3. Click New to add a new asset to the manifest.

4. From the Type drop-down list, select Microsoft.VisualStudio.MefComponent.

5. From the Source drop-down list, select A Project In Current Solution.

6. From the Project drop-down list, select the project that contained source.extension .vsixmanifest. At this point, the dialog box should look like this:

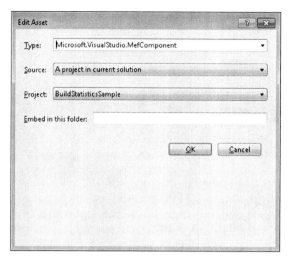

7. Click OK.

8. Save the manifest and close it.

We're now going to add a class to the Visual Studio package that represents our new Builds page section. Right-click the project; choose Add, Class; name the new class **BuildStatisticsSection**; and change its accessibility to **public.** You should end up with a class that looks like this:

```
using System;
using System.Collections.Generic;
using System.Linq;
using System.Text;
using System.Threading.Tasks;

namespace Company.BuildStatisticsSample
{
    public class BuildStatisticsSection
    {
    }
}
```

Next, we'll add the following namespace imports that we'll need:

■ Microsoft.TeamFoundation.Build.Client

■ Microsoft.TeamFoundation.Client

■ Microsoft.TeamFoundation.Controls

■ Microsoft.VisualStudio.TeamFoundation.Build

■ System.ComponentModel

Team Explorer uses attributes to discover page and section extensions. Next, we're going to apply the *TeamExplorerSection* attribute to our new class so that Team Explorer can discover it. This attribute takes the following three parameters:

- **An ID for the section.** This should be a GUID that is unique to your custom section (that is, if you create multiple sections, they should not share the same ID).

- **The ID of the page you want the section to appear on.** This is another GUID that identifies which Team Explorer page the section is a part of. The IDs for the built-in pages are available from Microsoft.TeamFoundation.Controls.TeamExplorerPageIds.

- **The priority of the section within that page.** This is an Int32 value that represents how the section should be sorted within the page, Team Explorer will show the sections in order of priority, so you can use this value to add your section at a specific location within the page.

We also need to implement the ITeamExplorerSection interface and property change notification so we can participate in the page's life cycle and expose the content that we want to display. Here's what the class now looks like (with changes shown in bold):

```csharp
using System;
using System.Collections.Generic;
using System.ComponentModel;
using System.Linq;
using System.Text;
using System.Threading.Tasks;
using Microsoft.TeamFoundation.Build.Client;
using Microsoft.TeamFoundation.Client;
using Microsoft.TeamFoundation.Controls;
using Microsoft.VisualStudio.TeamFoundation.Build;

namespace Company.BuildStatisticsSample
{
    [TeamExplorerSection("E52594FD-490A-4218-9D89-25B16500AA32", TeamExplorerPageIds.Builds,
10)]
    public class BuildStatisticsSection : ITeamExplorerSection
    {
        public BuildStatisticsSection()
        {
            Title = "Build Statistics";
            IsExpanded = true;
            IsVisible = true;
            IsBusy = false;
        }

        public void Cancel()
        {
        }

        public object GetExtensibilityService(Type serviceType)
        {
            return null;
        }

        private IServiceProvider m_ServiceProvider;
```

```csharp
public void Initialize(object sender, SectionInitializeEventArgs e)
{
    m_ServiceProvider = e.ServiceProvider;
}

private bool m_IsBusy;
public bool IsBusy
{
    get { return m_IsBusy; }
    private set { m_IsBusy = value; OnPropertyChanged("IsBusy"); }
}

private bool m_IsExpanded;
public bool IsExpanded
{
    get { return m_IsExpanded; }
    set { m_IsExpanded = value; OnPropertyChanged("IsExpanded"); }
}

private bool m_IsVisible;
public bool IsVisible
{
    get { return m_IsVisible; }
    set { m_IsVisible = value; OnPropertyChanged("IsVisible"); }
}

public void Loaded(object sender, SectionLoadedEventArgs e)
{
}

public void Refresh()
{
}

public void SaveContext(object sender, SectionSaveContextEventArgs e)
{
}

public object SectionContent
{
    get { return null; }
}

private string m_Title;
public string Title
{
    get { return m_Title; }
    private set { m_Title = value; OnPropertyChanged("Title"); }
}

public void Dispose()
{
}

public event PropertyChangedEventHandler PropertyChanged;
protected void OnPropertyChanged(string propertyName)
{
```

```
        if (PropertyChanged != null)
        {
            PropertyChanged(this, new PropertyChangedEventArgs(propertyName));
        }
    }
  }
}
```

At this point, if you debug the package (by clicking Debug, Start Debugging), it will start an experimental instance of Visual Studio; and if you connect to a Team Foundation Server and switch to the Builds page in Team Explorer, you'll see your new section, as shown in Figure 2-25.

FIGURE 2-25 A custom section in Team Explorer.

Stop debugging (by closing the experimental instance of Visual Studio), and now we'll add some static content to this section. To do this, create a user control that will contain our content as follows:

1. Right-click the project and choose Add, User Control. Name the user control BuildStatisticsSectionView and click Add.

2. Add a TextBlock with the text "Hello World" as a child of the *Grid* element, so that the XAML now looks like this:

```
<UserControl x:Class="Company.BuildStatisticsSample.BuildStatisticsSectionView"
             xmlns="http://schemas.microsoft.com/winfx/2006/xaml/presentation"
             xmlns:x="http://schemas.microsoft.com/winfx/2006/xaml"
             xmlns:mc="http://schemas.openxmlformats.org/markup-compatibility/2006"
             xmlns:d="http://schemas.microsoft.com/expression/blend/2008"
             mc:Ignorable="d"
             d:DesignHeight="300" d:DesignWidth="300">
    <Grid>
        <TextBlock Text="Hello World" />
    </Grid>
</UserControl>
```

3. Finally, modify the *BuildStatisticsSection* class by implementing the *SectionContent* property, adding a strongly typed wrapper property named *View,* and initializing the *SectionContent* property in the constructor:

```
public BuildStatisticsSection()
{
    Title = "Build Statistics";
    IsExpanded = true;
    IsVisible = true;
```

```
        IsBusy = false;
        SectionContent = new BuildStatisticsSectionView();
}


    private object m_View;
    public object SectionContent
    {
        get { return m_View; }
        private set { m_View = value; OnPropertyChanged("SectionContent"); }
    }

    public BuildStatisticsSectionView View
    {
        get { return SectionContent as BuildStatisticsSectionView; }
    }
```

Now if you start debugging again and switch to the Builds page in Team Explorer, you'll see that the section now contains the static content you added, as shown in Figure 2-26.

FIGURE 2-26 The custom section in Team Explorer showing static content.

Stop debugging again, and now we'll modify the section to display some dynamic content instead of the static content. Do this by performing the following steps:

1. Open the BuildStatisticsSectionView user control code-behind file (by right-clicking it and choosing View Code).

2. Modify the constructor to set DataContext to the current class. It should look like this:

```
public BuildStatisticsSectionView()
{
    InitializeComponent();
    DataContext = this;
}
```

3. Add a dependency property that we can use to pass information into this view. For this example, we're going to add an integer that represents the number of builds that have completed in the last hour:

```
public int RecentlyCompletedBuildCount
{
    get { return (int)GetValue(RecentlyCompletedBuildCountProperty); }
    set { SetValue(RecentlyCompletedBuildCountProperty, value); }
}
```

```
public static readonly DependencyProperty RecentlyCompletedBuildCountProperty =
    DependencyProperty.Register("RecentlyCompletedBuildCount", typeof(int),
    typeof(BuildStatisticsSectionView), new PropertyMetadata(0));
```

4. Switch to the design view by right-clicking the file in Solution Explorer and clicking View Designer.

5. Replace the Hello World TextBlock added earlier with the following code:

```
<StackPanel Orientation="Horizontal">
    <TextBlock VerticalAlignment="Top" Margin="0,0,4,0">Recently Completed Builds:</
TextBlock>
    <TextBlock VerticalAlignment="Top" Text="{Binding RecentlyCompletedBuildCount}" />
</StackPanel>
```

6. Save and close the BuildStatisticsSectionView.xaml file and open the *BuildStatisticsSection* class so we can implement the business logic to update the view.

7. Modify *Initialize* to call the *Refresh* method so that a refresh will be forced when the *Initialize* method is called by Team Explorer:

```
public void Initialize(object sender, SectionInitializeEventArgs e)
{
    m_ServiceProvider = e.ServiceProvider;
    Refresh();
}
```

8. Add an asynchronous method to perform a refresh. In this example, we're querying the current team project (determined using the ITeamFoundationContextManager service) to find how many builds have completed in the last hour, and then passing that count to the dependency property on the view that was created earlier:

```
public async Task RefreshAsync()
{
    try
    {
        IsBusy = true;

        var contextManager = (ITeamFoundationContextManager)m_ServiceProvider.
GetService(
            typeof(ITeamFoundationContextManager));
        var buildService = (IVsTeamFoundationBuild)m_ServiceProvider.GetService(
            typeof(IVsTeamFoundationBuild));
        var buildServer = buildService.BuildServer;

        var buildDetailSpec = buildServer.CreateBuildDetailSpec(
            contextManager.CurrentContext.TeamProjectName);
        buildDetailSpec.Status = BuildStatus.All ^
            BuildStatus.InProgress ^ BuildStatus.NotStarted; //Only completed builds
        buildDetailSpec.MinFinishTime = DateTime.Now.AddHours(-1);

        //Performance optimizations
        buildDetailSpec.InformationTypes = new string[] { };
```

```
    buildDetailSpec.QueryOptions = QueryOptions.None;

    IBuildQueryResult buildQueryResult = null;
    await Task.Run(() =>
    {
        buildQueryResult = buildServer.QueryBuilds(buildDetailSpec);
    });

    View.RecentlyCompletedBuildCount = buildQueryResult.Builds.Length;
}
finally
{
    IsBusy = false;
}
}
```

9. Modify the implementation of *ITeamExplorerSection.Refresh* to call the *RefreshAsync* method:

```
public async void Refresh()
{
    await RefreshAsync();
}
```

Now when you start debugging and switch to the Builds page in Team Explorer, you should see the number of recently completed builds (as shown in Figure 2-27), and this will refresh the view each time you click the Refresh button at the top of the Team Explorer window.

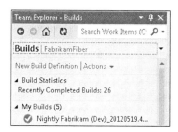

FIGURE 2-27 A custom section in Team Explorer showing dynamic content.

CHAPTER 3

What's new in web publishing

In Microsoft Visual Studio 2010, the MSBuild-based web publishing experience was introduced for Web Application Projects (including both ASP.NET MVC and Web Forms). Along with that release came the foundation for the wave of updates that are included with Visual Studio 2012. The Visual Studio web team is also releasing regular updates to the web publishing experience, along with ASP.NET updates and changes to the Azure software development kit (SDK). The updated web publishing experience has been made available for Visual Studio 2010 SP1 as well. You can install the latest web publishing support, including both Visual Studio 2012 and 2010 SP1, from the Azure SDK, which you can find at *http://www.windowsazure.com*.

Since Visual Studio 2012 was initially released, there have already been a few updates to the web publishing experience. At this time, the latest Azure SDK is version 1.8. The content in this chapter has been written on the assumption that the Azure SDK 1.8 has been installed. We will highlight any new content that is not built into Visual Studio 2012. For the remainder of the chapter, we will discuss the updates in terms of Visual Studio 2012, but all the material also applies to Visual Studio 2010 with the Azure SDK.

Overview of the new Publish Web dialog box

In Visual Studio 2010, the Publish Web dialog box was pretty basic. It had some profile management options at the top and minimal publishing settings. You can see the Publish Web dialog box from Visual Studio 2010 in Figure 3-1.

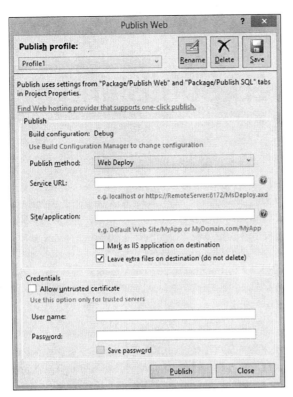

FIGURE 3-1 The Visual Studio 2010 Publish Web dialog box.

In Visual Studio 2012, the Publish Web dialog box has been extensively updated. The dialog box now consists of several different tabs. Even though the dialog box has more functionality, the overall experience is simpler. This is especially the case when the Import functionality is used to populate the settings. In Figure 3-2, you can see the new Publish Web dialog box.

The Publish Web dialog box consists of four tabs. On the Profile tab, you can manage your profiles. To create a new profile, you can either click Import and select an existing *.publishSettings* file, or you can create a new profile manually by selecting the New option from the Select Or Import A Publish Profile drop-down list. A *.publishSettings* file is a simple XML file that contains the publishing information. This file is produced by many web hosting providers and can be used with Visual Studio or Web Matrix. If your hosting provider does not make these files available, you should demand that they do. These *.publishSettings* files are different from the *.pubxml* files created with Visual Studio. The *.pubxml* files contain the remote endpoint information, as well as values that are specific to the publishing requirements of your project. In contrast, the *.publishSettings* file just contains the publishing endpoint information. The other difference is that a *.publishSettings* file can contain more than one set of publish settings. For example, Windows Azure Web Sites includes both a Web Deploy profile and the File Transfer Protocol (FTP) settings.

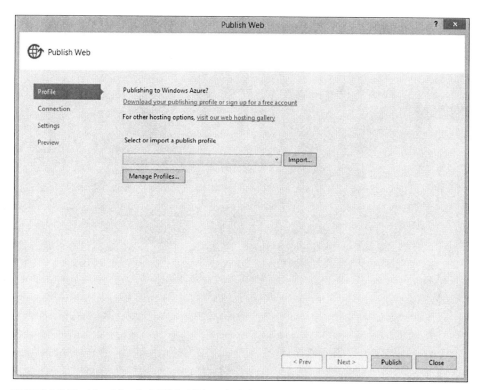

FIGURE 3-2 The Visual Studio 2012 Publish Web dialog box.

Here is a basic publishing scenario: You have an existing ASP.NET project that you need to publish to a remote web host. Your host provides a *.publishSettings* file, which you can import into Visual Studio. In my case, I'm publishing to Windows Azure Web Sites, but this flow works for any hosting provider that supports *.publishSettings* files. To open the Publish Web dialog box, right-click the web project in Solution Explorer and select Publish, which will open the dialog box shown in Figure 3-2. You can use the Import button to import the *.publishSettings* file. After importing the file, you will be brought to the Connection tab automatically. You can see this tab in Figure 3-3.

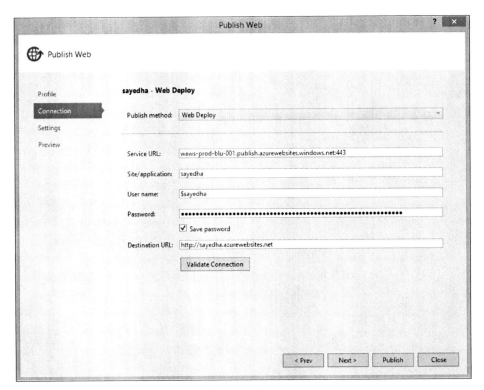

FIGURE 3-3 The Connection tab of the Publish Web dialog box.

The values from the *.publishSettings* file are used to populate all the settings on the Connection tab. Depending on your hosting provider, you may need to specify the User Name and Password information here. You can also click Validate Connection to double-check that all the settings are correct. We will discuss the Connection tab in more detail when we demonstrate creating a package in the "Building web packages" section later in this chapter. The next tab in this dialog box is the Settings tab, shown in Figure 3-4.

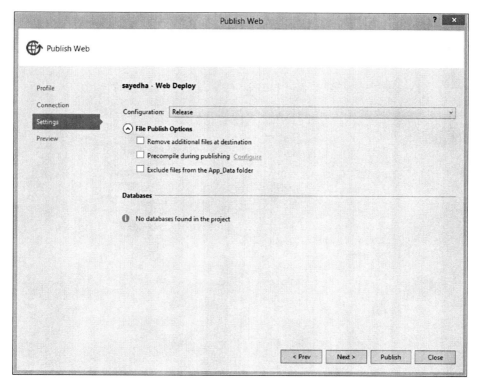

FIGURE 3-4 The Settings tab of the Publish Web dialog box.

On this tab, you can specify the build configuration that should be used during publishing by choosing an item from the Configuration drop-down list. When you configure this value, keep in mind that these values are drawn from the project build configurations, not solution build configurations. If you expect to see an additional value in the drop-down list but do not, odds are that you created a solution build configuration, but not a corresponding project build configuration. You can fix this by using the Configuration Manager in Visual Studio. One thing to be aware of with respect to this value: it's used only for the Visual Studio publishing process. For command-line scenarios, you need to specify the value for Configuration, as you would for any other build. Sayed has a good blog post with more details at *http://sedodream.com/2012/10/27/MSBuildHowToSetTheConfigurationProperty.aspx*. After you click Next, you will be taken to the Preview tab.

On the Preview tab, you can see the operations that will be performed when you publish your application. There are two areas: Files and Databases. In Figure 3-5, you can see the Preview tab populated with data from the SampleWeb project.

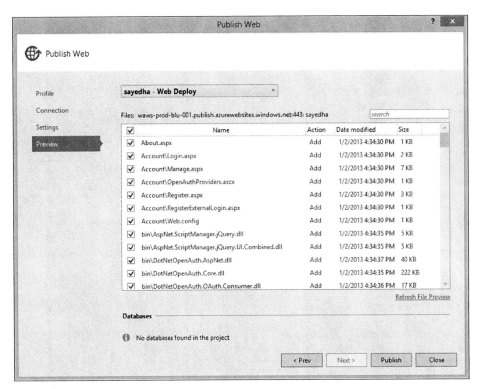

FIGURE 3-5 The Preview tab of the Publish Web dialog box.

> **Note** You can double-click a file to see the difference between the local file and the remote file.

Because this project, SampleWeb, does not contain any databases, you only see file-related operations. When dealing with files, there are three possible Action types: *Add, Update,* and *Delete*. Because I've never published this project before, all the Action values are set to *Add*. At this point, we are ready to go, so click Publish to start the process. You can monitor the progress in the output window. After publishing your project, if a value was provided for the Destination URL on the Connection tab, that URL will be opened in a browser after a successful publish. Now that you have been introduced to the Publish Web dialog box, let's discuss how to create a web package in Visual Studio 2012.

Building web packages

In Visual Studio 2012, you may have noticed that a menu option, Build Deployment Package, has disappeared. Don't worry—it's still easy to create a package. To create a web package in Visual Studio 2012, you can use the Publish Web dialog box. When you open the Publish Web dialog box, you can create a new profile on the Profile tab. To do that, use the New option in the Select Or Import A Publish Profile drop-down list. On the Connection tab, select Web Deploy Package from the Publish

Method drop-down list. There are many benefits to using a publish profile for packaging, some of which include the following:

1. Packages can include database artifacts.

2. You can customize the package process by using the *.pubxml* file.

3. You can package from the command line in the same way that you publish.

When you create the package profile in the Publish Web dialog box, the Connection tab will look like Figure 3-6.

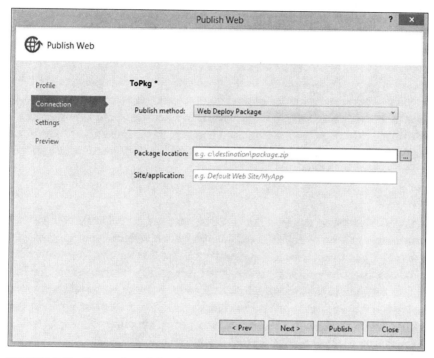

FIGURE 3-6 The Connection tab for the package profile.

In Figure 3-6, you can see two input fields: Package Location and Site/Application. Package Location should contain the path to the *.zip* file that you want to produce. This is a required field. The value for Site/Application is optional, but if you know the website or application that you are publishing to, you can provide the site name or application path here. When the package is published, this value will be used for the Web Deploy parameter *IIS Web Application Name*. Now let's create a package and take a look at the *.pubxml* file that was created.

Included in the samples is the PackageSample project. If you open that project, you will see that a package profile is defined. This profile, like other profiles, is stored in the PublishProfiles folder under Properties (My Project for Microsoft Visual Basic). Here are the contents of the ToPkg.pubxml file:

```
<Project ToolsVersion="4.0"
        xmlns="http://schemas.microsoft.com/developer/msbuild/2003">
```

```
<PropertyGroup>
  <WebPublishMethod>Package</WebPublishMethod>
  <SiteUrlToLaunchAfterPublish />
  <DesktopBuildPackageLocation>
      C:\InsideMSBuild\PublishOutput\PkgSample-default\PackageSample.zip
  </DesktopBuildPackageLocation>
  <PackageAsSingleFile>true</PackageAsSingleFile>
  <DeployIisAppPath />
  <PublishDatabaseSettings>
    <Objects xmlns="" />
  </PublishDatabaseSettings>
</PropertyGroup>
</Project>
```

In this profile, you can see that *WebPublishMethod* is set to *Package,* which indicates that this is a profile that can be used to create a package. The path for the package is stored as the MSBuild property *DesktopBuildPackageLocation.* The other notable item here is the *PublishDatabaseSettings* property. Because my application did not contain any databases, this property is essentially empty. Even though it is empty, you should not remove it from the *.pubxml* file. You can easily automate the process of creating a package by following the same technique you use to automate the publishing process. Specifically, you'll create a publish profile and then use it to automate the process. Let's now take a closer look at publish profiles, including how to use them to automate packaging and publishing.

Publish profiles

When using the Publish Web dialog box after publishing or packaging, a publish profile is created. The publish profile contains all the settings entered into the Publish Web dialog box, as well as options that have not yet been seen in the dialog box. We can use these profiles from either Visual Studio or the command line. After your first publish profile is created, when you reopen the Publish Web dialog box, you are taken to the Preview tab with the most recently used profile automatically selected. On the Preview tab, you can switch profiles quickly using the drop-down list at the top of the dialog box. If you need to publish to a new destination, just go back to the Profile tab and create a new profile. You can have as many profiles defined as you like.

Publish profiles are saved in a folder named PublishProfiles under Properties (My Project for Visual Basic projects). Each profile will be saved into its own file with the extension of *.pubxml.* These files will be added to the project, and to source control, by default. Your publishing password will be saved in a *.user* file, which can only be decrypted by you, and not checked into version control, so you don't have to worry about any unauthorized publishing actions. If you want to keep a profile out of the sight of others, you can simply exclude the *.pubxml* file from the project and source control. When the Publish Web dialog box is opened, it will inspect the folder for the list of all profiles, not just profiles that are a part of the project. Now let's take a closer look at a sample *.pubxml* file.

In the following code block, you will see the contents of a Visual Studio publish profile that was created when I imported a *.publishSettings* file (these files are provided by hosting companies):

```
<Project ToolsVersion="4.0" xmlns="http://schemas.microsoft.com/developer/msbuild/2003">
  <PropertyGroup>
    <WebPublishMethod>MSDeploy</WebPublishMethod>
```

```
    <LastUsedBuildConfiguration>Release</LastUsedBuildConfiguration>
    <LastUsedPlatform>Any CPU</LastUsedPlatform>
    <SiteUrlToLaunchAfterPublish>http://sayedha.azurewebsites.net</SiteUrlToLaunchAfterPublish>
    <ExcludeApp_Data>False</ExcludeApp_Data>
    <MSDeployServiceURL>
        waws-prod-blu-001.publish.azurewebsites.windows.net:443</MSDeployServiceURL>
    <DeployIisAppPath>sayedha</DeployIisAppPath>
    <SkipExtraFilesOnServer>True</SkipExtraFilesOnServer>
    <MSDeployPublishMethod>WMSVC</MSDeployPublishMethod>
    <EnableMSDeployBackup>True</EnableMSDeployBackup>
    <UserName>$sayedha</UserName>
    <_SavePWD>True</_SavePWD>
  </PropertyGroup>
</Project>
```

From this code block, you can see that the *.pubxml* file is an MSBuild file. The properties declared are specific to the publishing method that is being used. Each *.pubxml* file has a single profile and contains all the values that are used by the Publish Web dialog box for this particular profile. This file is used by the Visual Studio user interface, but you can also employ this from the command line. Command-line publishing is supported only for the following publishing methods: Web Deploy, Web Deploy Package, and File System.

Web publish profiles are designed to allow you to extend the build and publishing process for a given publishing operation. When a publish profile is used to publish your application, the publish profile will be imported into the project itself. Because the *.pubxml* file is imported into the project file, you have full access to all MSBuild properties and items defined in the project. Because of this, from the *.pubxml* file, you can customize the build process and the publishing process. From the second edition, you may remember that you could customize the publishing process by editing the *.wpp.targets* file. Let's look at how to use this profile to publish the project from the command line.

Automating web publishing using a publish profile

Publishing from the command line is much easier than it used to be. If you remember from Chapter 19, "Web deployment tool practical applications," when publishing from the command prompt, you were required to pass in about 10 properties. Let's take a look at how simple the new command can be. This command can be used to publish SampleWeb using the profile *named to-prod*:

```
msbuild SampleWeb.sln /p:DeployOnBuild=true /p:PublishProfile=to-prod /p:Password=<insert-
password>
```

> **Note** Depending on the web host that you are publishing to, you may need to also add /p:AllowUntrustedCertificate=true.

> **Tip** If you are building a Visual Studio project file instead of the solution file, you should also specify the value for /p:VisualStudioVersion=11.0. Without this, the default value of 10.0 will be used.

With this command, the solution file will be built and published. When the *DeployOnBuild* property is set to *True*, the build process will be extended to publish the project as well. The name of the publish profile is passed in as the *PublishProfile* property. When specifying the value for *PublishProfile*, you have two options. You can pass in the name of the profile, in which case the build will use the named profile from the default location, or you can pass in the file path to the *.pubxml* file. Now let's look at how to use this same approach to create packages.

Automating web packaging using a publish profile

You can use this same technique when creating a package from the command line. The PackageSample project has a profile named ToPkg, which will create the web deploy package at C:\InsideMSBuild\ PublishOutput\PkgSample-default\PackageSample.zip. In order to create this from the command line, we can execute the following command when building the project:

```
msbuild PackageSample.csproj /p:DeployOnBuild=true /p:PublishProfile=ToPkg
/p:VisualStudioVersion=11.0
```

With this command, you can override specific properties as well. For example, we showed previously that the package location is stored in the *.pubxml* file as an MSBuild property, *DesktopBuildPackageLocation*. If you would like to override the location where the package is created, pass the property as a command-line argument. For example, if I wanted to publish the package to C:\Temp\AltDest\Mypackage.zip, you can use the following command (which shows the value for *DesktopBuildPackageLocation* in bold).

```
msbuild PackageSample.csproj /p:DeployOnBuild=true /p:PublishProfile=ToPkg
/p:VisualStudioVersion=11.0 /p:DesktopBuildPackageLocation=c:\temp\altDest\mypackage.zip
```

Because the *DesktopBuildPackageLocation* property is specified as a command-line parameter, it overrides the value in the *.pubxml* file. Following the execution of this command, the package is written to the location provided. Now that we've shown how you can publish and package from the command line using a publish profile, we will discuss how the *.pubxml* file relates to the *.wpp.targets* file.

Relationship between publish profiles and *.wpp.targets*

In the second edition of this book, we showed how to customize the publishing process by creating a file named *{ProjectName}*.wpp.targets in the root of your project folder. The support for importing the *.wpp.targets* file has been in place since Visual Studio 2010. When a web project is built, it will look for a file in the same folder as the project file, with the naming pattern *{ProjectName}*.wpp.targets. If the file exists, it will be imported using the MSBuild *Import* element. This is very similar to how publish profiles work. There is one significant difference though. The *.wpp.targets* file will be imported for *every build*, not just for publishing. Because of this, you have to be a bit more careful, as it may affect other scenarios besides publishing.

For publishing customizations, it's recommended that you place those customizations inside the publish profile instead of a *.wpp.targets* file. This is because the modifications will only affect that particular publish profile, and it is much easier for others to diagnose any issues with publishing. Not many users would think to check for a *.wpp.targets* file if there are publishing issues.

You should use a *.wpp.targets* file if one of the following conditions exists:

- You want to extend the build process.

- You want to extend the publishing process for all publish profiles.

If you have existing projects with a *.wpp.targets* file, you do not need to modify them. They will continue to work. For new projects, you should place publish customizations in the publish profile. Let's move on to discuss the database support that exists in the web publish support.

Database publishing support

With the release of Visual Studio 2012, you now have the ability to publish database artifacts incrementally. Visual Studio has support for publishing databases in two ways: using Entity Framework (EF) Code First migrations and using a data-tier application package (DACPAC). We will first discuss EF Code First support and then discuss DACPAC support.

EF Code First migrations

If you have a web application that uses EF Code First, the recommended method to publish its database artifacts is to use EF Code First migrations. As you change your web application's database model, those changes are captured in code called *migrations*. When executed, migrations make the necessary changes to the database, thus keeping your database model and database in sync. You can easily move from one version of your database model to another by executing those migrations. Let's take a quick look at how EF Code First migrations work and then we will describe the support offered by the Publish Web dialog box.

When using EF Code First, you will create a context class, which you will use to access your database. After creating your context class, you will create one or more migration classes using the Package Manager Console. There are two ways to execute these migrations against a database: by using the Package Manager Console and by executing them at run time. The Publish Web dialog box involves the latter mechanism. You can configure your application to execute migrations at run time in two ways: by adding some code to your project to invoke the migrations, or by adding some elements to the Web.config file. The Publish Web dialog box uses the second approach to enable the migrations. Let's take a closer look at that.

If you have a web project with EF Code First contexts (classes extending DbContext), when you open the Publish Web dialog box, you will see those contexts on the Settings tab. Figure 3-7 shows what the dialog box looks like when you have an EF Code First context in your project but there are no migrations associated with it.

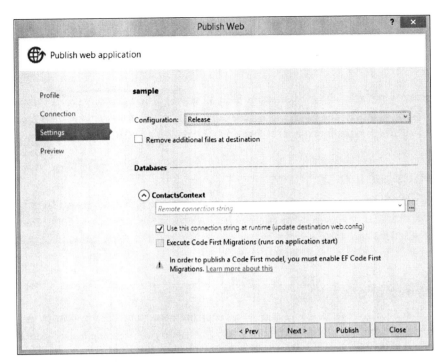

FIGURE 3-7 No mitigations are associated with your project.

In Figure 3-7, you can see the *ContactsContext* class on the Settings tab of the Publish Web dialog box. In this case, there is a message indicating that you will need to create EF Code First migrations to publish the database associated with the context. Once you add migrations for the context, then the Execute Code First Migrations check box will be enabled. After adding a migration, when you re-enter the Publish Web dialog box, you can enter a destination connection string and enable the migrations to be executed. The connection string provided will be used for executing both the migrations and the run-time connection string.

Tip If you have a project with an EF Code First context and do not see it in the Publish Web dialog box, close the dialog box, rebuild the project, and then reopen the dialog box.

When you publish or package your web project, the final Web.config file will have the elements required to invoke the migrations. The migrations will be executed the first time that the EF Code First context is accessed. If your Web.config file does not have a connection string entry for the EF Code First context, then one will be added automatically to the published Web.config file. Now that we have discussed EF Code First contexts, let's move on to discuss the DACPAC support that is built in.

Incremental database publishing with DACPACs

If you need to publish the schema for a database incrementally, you can use a DAC package, also known as a *DACPAC*. A DACPAC is defined as follows in the MSDN library:

> A DAC is a self-contained unit of SQL Server database deployment that enables
> data-tier developers and database administrators to package SQL Server objects into
> a portable artifact called a DAC package, also known as a DACPAC.

In other words, a DACPAC contains all the schema artifacts that the database consists of. The significance of the words *portable artifact* should be highlighted here. The aspect that makes a DACPAC portable is the incremental publish support that is built on top of it. When using a DACPAC during publish time, the schema captured in the DACPAC is compared to that of the target database. The publish process will compute the difference between the DACPAC and the target database and then execute the difference against the target database. If the two are equal, then a no-op will be performed. Let's see how this works during the Publish Web workflow.

When you open the Publish Web dialog box, if you have any connection strings in the Web.config file that are not associated with an EF Code First context, then you will see those on the Settings tab. For example, in Figure 3-8, you can see the Settings tab for the ContactsSample project.

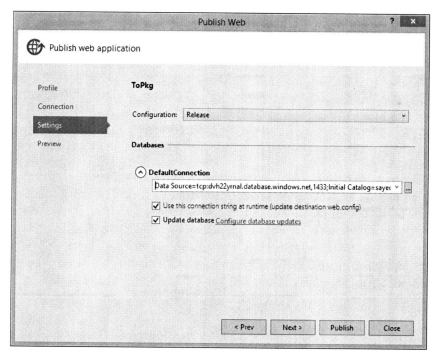

FIGURE 3-8 The Publish Web dialog box with a database selected for publishing.

When you check the Update Database check box on the Settings tab when your web project is published or packaged, a DACPAC is created from the source connection string. This DACPAC is then transferred to the remote server to publish the database-related artifacts. This is facilitated by the new dbDacFx Web Deploy provider. This process is depicted in Figure 3-9.

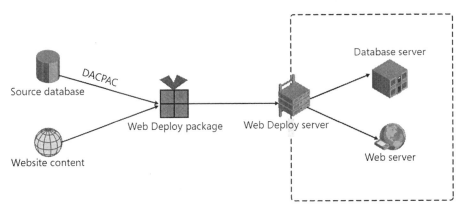

FIGURE 3-9 A Web and DACPAC publishing diagram.

In Figure 3-9, you can see that a DACPAC is created from the source database and placed in a Web Deploy package (or a folder for the direct publish case), and the web content is also placed there. The database schema will be published first, followed by any web updates. Both of these processes will be incremental; that is, only the changes will be applied, not a full publish. In Figure 3-9, the dotted line represents a firewall that may be in place. When publishing, if you do not have direct access to the remote database (which is common for many cloud hosting providers by default), that is OK so long as the Web Deploy server has access to it. When creating a Web Deploy package, the DACPAC will be placed inside the package and Web Deploy parameters will be created so that you can update the connection string during publishing. We will now discuss how to create a Web Deploy package with a DACPAC.

In the samples, you will find the ContactsSample project, which is a basic web application that stores contacts in a Microsoft SQL Server database. When creating a package for this on the Settings tab, I've chosen to package the database and provide a default connection string as well. This was shown previously in Figure 3-8. The resulting package will have the DACPAC for the source database in the root of the package. Let's see what happens when you import this package using the Microsoft IIS Manager user interface. Using IIS Manager, you can right-click a site and then select Import Application under the Deploy menu to import a Web Deploy package (see Figure 3-10).

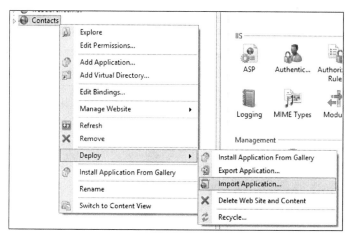

FIGURE 3-10 The Import Application option is the IIS Manager.

  Tip If you do not see the Import Application option, you need to install Web Deploy with the IIS Manager Extensions option checked.

After selecting the package to be imported, you will be prompted to fill in the values for the Web Deploy parameters (as shown in Figure 3-11).

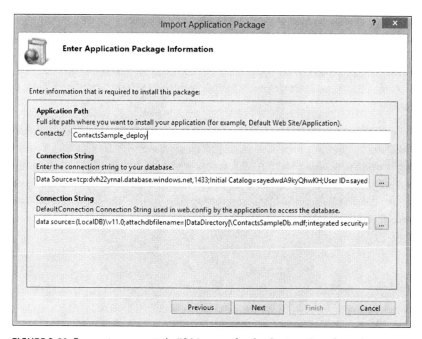

FIGURE 3-11 Parameter prompts in IIS Manager for the ContactsSample package.

In Figure 3-11, you can see three parameters. The first parameter will define the IIS App path where your application will be installed. The next two parameters are connection strings for the DACPAC. The first is for the connection string used to publish the database related artifacts, and the final one is for the run-time connection string that goes in the Web.config file. If you want to use a lower-privileged connection string at run time, you can do so. After clicking Next, the database publish operations will be performed, followed by an update of the site itself. Now that we've discussed database publishing with DACPACs, let discuss the updates that are available for Web.config transforms.

Profile-specific Web.config transforms

In Visual Studio 2010, Web.config transforms were introduced, which you can use to update the Web.config file during the publish/package operation. If you are rusty on the basics of transforms, take a look back at Chapter 18, "Web deployment tool, part 2," in the second edition. In Visual Studio 2010, these transforms were tied to the build configuration. If you published using the Release build configuration, then the Web.config file would be transformed using Web.release.config. In Visual Studio 2012, you can now also have profile-specific transforms. A convention is used to associate a profile with a specific transform. To have a Web.config transform for a given profile, create a file with the pattern web.*{ProfileName}*.config next to Web.config. When the file is detected, it will be applied after the build configuration transform. You can see the Web.config transforms in Figure 3-12.

Source   Web.*{Buildconfig}*.config   Web.*{Profile}*.config   Final
Web.config   Web.config

FIGURE 3-12 A Web.config transformation illustration.

When the Web.config file is being transformed, if either the build configuration transform or the profile-specific transform does not exist, that particular transform will simply be skipped. Let's take a look at how this works.

When Visual Studio 2012 was initially released, the underlying support to invoke these transforms existed in the web MSBuild targets, but there was no way to create these transforms easily. You had to create the transforms manually. In the ASP.NET 2012.2 update for Visual Studio 2012, a new context menu was added to help you create these transforms. With this update, you can create a profile-specific transform easily by right-clicking the *.pubxml* file and selecting Add Config Transform. You can see this new menu option in Figure 3-13.

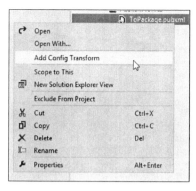

FIGURE 3-13 The Add Config Transform menu option for publish profiles.

When you invoke the Add Config Transform command, it will create the Web.config transform in the root of the project with the correct name and open it automatically. In the samples, you will find a project, TransformSample, that contains the ToPackage.pubxml publish profile. This publish profile is used when creating a web deploy package for this project. In this project, we have created the following transforms:

- Web.debug.config

- Web.release.config

- Web.ToPackage.config

Along with the Web.config file, the contents of these transforms are shown next. We will leave off the Web.debug.config file because it is not used in this demo.

Web.config file
```
<configuration>

  <appSettings>
    <add key="default" value="default"/>
  </appSettings>

    <system.web>
      <compilation debug="true" targetFramework="4.0" />
    </system.web>

</configuration>
```

Web.release.config
```
<configuration xmlns:xdt="http://schemas.microsoft.com/XML-Document-Transform">
  <appSettings>
    <add key="release" value="from-release" xdt:Transform="Insert"/>
  </appSettings>

  <system.web>
    <compilation xdt:Transform="RemoveAttributes(debug)" />
  </system.web>
</configuration>
```

Web.ToPackage.config

```
<configuration xmlns:xdt="http://schemas.microsoft.com/XML-Document-Transform">

  <appSettings>
    <add key="to-package" value="from-ToPackage-transform" xdt:Transform="Insert"/>
  </appSettings>

</configuration>
```

The Web.release.config transform adds a new *appSettings* entry named *release* and removes the *debug* attribute from the compilation element. The Web.ToPackage.config transform adds a new *appSettings* entry named *to-package*. Packaging the application using the ToPackage profile produces the following Web.config file:

Final web.config after transforms

```
<configuration>

  <appSettings>
    <add key="default" value="default"/>
    <add key="release" value="from-release"/>
    <add key="to-package" value="from-ToPackage-transform"/>
  </appSettings>

  <system.web>
    <compilation targetFramework="4.0" />
  </system.web>

</configuration>
```

In this file, you can see that the release transform inserted the release app setting and removed the *debug* attribute from the *compilation* element. You can also see that the Web.ToPackage.config transform was invoked. Another subtle thing to notice here is the order in which the app settings were inserted. The release setting was inserted before the *to-package* element. This indicates that the Web.release.config transform was invoked before Web.ToPackage.config.

Another feature released with Visual Studio 2012 is the ability to preview these transforms. In Visual Studio 2010, if you wanted to see the resulting Web.config transform, you would have to either publish or package your project, which made developing these transforms much more difficult than it should have been. In Visual Studio 2012, however, you can now preview Web.config transforms easily. The preview functionality works for build configuration transforms as well as profile-specific ones. You can right-click and select Preview Transform on any of the transforms. This new option is shown in Figure 3-14.

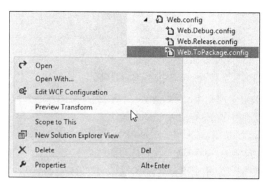

FIGURE 3-14 The Preview Transform menu option.

Once you invoke this preview, you will be able to see the final Web.config transform. When you preview a profile-specific transform, it will invoke the correct build configuration transform before applying the profile-specific one. It mimics the behavior that it will show when publishing. When you are viewing the preview results, you can see which transforms have been applied in the upper-right corner (see Figure 3-15).

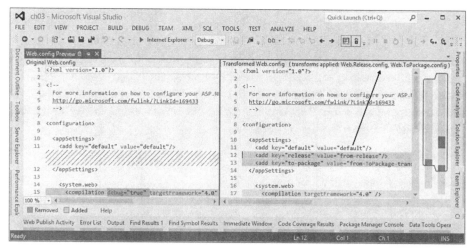

FIGURE 3-15 A Web.config transform preview.

With these updates for Web.config transforms, it's much easier to create and use Web.config transforms. This concludes the Web.config transform content, as well as the section covering the new features. We will now move on to look at some real-world examples.

Cookbook

How to publish a package to multiple destinations

One of the most common questions that I'm asked is, "How can I create a Web Deploy package that can be used to publish to multiple servers?" Any Web Deploy package can be published to any destination, but you may need to tweak the content for the destination. This is particularly true for Web.config. One of the challenges when creating a package from Visual Studio that can target multiple destinations is the handling of Web.config. When you create a package in Visual Studio or from the command line, the Web.config that is placed in the resulting package is already transformed. This makes these packages difficult to publish to multiple different locations by default. There is an extension created by Sayed that can help here, called PackageWeb.

PackageWeb can be used to help create portable packages that can be published easily to multiple destinations. PackageWeb is a *NuGet* package that can be installed into web projects. Let's see how PackageWeb works. To use PackageWeb, you will need to add the package to your web project. You can do this either from the Manage NuGet Packages dialog box or from the Package Manager Console. From the Package Manager Console, you can execute the following command:

```
Install-Package PackageWeb
```

Once the package has been installed in your project, it will extend the package process. When you create a package after installing PackageWeb, you will see a new file, Publish-Interactive.ps1, in the output location. This is a Windows PowerShell script that can be used to publish this package. From a PowerShell prompt, you can invoke this script to start the publish process. Once you invoke this script, you will be prompted for the following set of values:

- Web.config transform to execute
- Web Deploy publish settings
- Web Deploy parameter values

After providing these values, the Web.config file will be transformed with the given transform and the publish operation will be invoked. Let's see this in action. In the samples, the project PkgWebDemo already has PackageWeb installed. After creating the package, you can invoke Publish-Interactive.ps1 to start the publish process. Figure 3-16 shows PackageWeb prompts for the Web Deploy publish settings. Because there are no Web Deploy parameters created for the sample, you are not prompted for those.

```
Now collecting parameters for publishing
You can press <enter> to go with default values
For an empty string use a single space
Parameter names in green
Default parameter values in cyan
*****************************************************************************
IIS Web Application Name: Default Web Site/PkgWebDemo_deploy
    new value>sayedwebdb
Computer name: localhost
    new value>waws-prod-bay-001.publish.azurewebsites.windows.net:443
Username:
    new value>$sayedwebdb
Password:
    new value>************************************************************
Allow untrusted certificate: false
    new value>true
whatif: false
    new value>true
MSDeploy command:
"C:\Program Files\IIS\Microsoft Web Deploy V3\msdeploy.exe" -verb:sync -source:archiveDir="C:\Users\sayedha\AppData\Local\Temp\Pkg
WebDemo_zip" -dest:auto,includeAcls='False',ComputerName='https://waws-prod-bay-001.publish.azurewebsites.windows.net:443/msdeploy
.axd?site=sayedwebdb',Username=$sayedwebdb,Password=3************************,AuthType='BASIC'
-disableLink:AppPoolExtension -disableLink:ContentExtension -disableLink:CertificateExtension -setParamFile:"C:\Users\sayedha\AppD
ata\Local\Temp\PkgWebDemo_zip\SetParameters.xml" -whatif -skip:objectName=dirPath,absolutePath="_Deploy_" -skip:objectName=filePat
h,absolutePath=web\..*\.config -skip:objectName=dirPath,absolutePath=_Package -skip:objectName=filePath,absolutePath=.*\.wpp\.targ
ets$ -allowUntrusted -enableRule:DoNotDelete
```

FIGURE 3-16 PackageWeb prompts for the Web Deploy settings.

After completing the prompts, Msdeploy.exe is called to start the publish process. In Figure 3-16, you can see the call to Msdeploy.exe that is invoked. The password value in this image is blurred for security reasons. Once you fill in the prompts and publish your package, a new file, PublishConfiguration .ps1.readme, will be created in the same folder. This file contains all the values for the prompts that were entered. The only value not persisted is the password; you will need to update this value manually. In order for PakageWeb to pick up this file automatically, just remove the *.readme* extension.

When PackageWeb is invoked, it will look for a file named PublishConfiguration.ps1 in the same folder as the Publish-Interactive.ps1 file. If that file exists, it will be imported, and you will not be prompted for values. (This is a very brief discussion of PackageWeb; for more details visit *http://msbuildbook.com/packageweb*.) Let's move on to discuss a neat trick that you can use during the package process.

Customizing the folder structure inside the package

When you create a package in Visual Studio by default, the full source structure is replicated inside the package. For example, when packaging the PackageSample project using the ToPkg profile, you can see how the contents are structured in the resulting *.zip* file in Figure 3-17.

FIGURE 3-17 The default folder structure for the PackageSample project.

In Figure 3-17, you can see that the source folder structure is replicated inside the generated PackageSample.zip file. This behavior is annoying, but it can go beyond that and cause real difficulties if you need to expand this package. When publishing with Web Deploy, the depth of these folders does not matter, but if you expand them on disk and manipulate the files, you may exceed the maximum path length. To avoid this, it would be better to create a Web Deploy package that did not have these unnecessary folders. Let's see what it would take to simplify the folder structure here.

When creating a package using web projects, the following basic steps are followed:

1. Build a project.

2. Gather all files in a Temp directory.

3. Create the package by calling Web Deploy.

Step 3 is executed by creating an XML file that describes how to create the package. This is referred to as a *Source Manifest file*. You can find this file in the same folder in which the package is created. If you inspect the file generated when packaging the PackageSample project, you will find the contents to be as shown in the following code block:

```xml
<?xml version="1.0" encoding="utf-8"?>
<sitemanifest>
  <IisApp path="C:\InsideMSBuild\ch03\PackageSample\obj\Release\Package\PackageTmp"
                managedRuntimeVersion="v4.0" />
  <setAcl path="C:\InsideMSBuild\ch03\PackageSample\obj\Release\Package\PackageTmp"
                setAclResourceType="Directory" />
  <setAcl path="C:\InsideMSBuild\ch03\PackageSample\obj\Release\Package\PackageTmp"
                setAclUser="anonymousAuthenticationUser" setAclResourceType="Directory" />
</sitemanifest>
```

In this manifest, you can see that three Web Deploy providers will be called when the package is created. Each of these providers references the full path to the temporary package folder. These are the values shown in bold in this code, and this is what we want to update during the package creation process. You can see the goal in Figure 3-18.

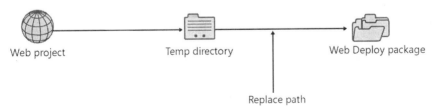

FIGURE 3-18 The process to update file paths for the generated package.

As you can see, we will replace the path *during* the package operation. We will do this with a Web Deploy replace rule. Let's see how to do that with some customizations to the *.pubxml* file.

When creating a package using Web Projects, you have the ability to replace values as the .zip file is being created. This is facilitated by using a replace rule. The replace rule that we want to create should match the package path and replace it with a much simpler value. To add a Web Deploy replace rule, you need to populate the MSDeployReplaceRules item list in the .pubxml file before the package is created. The next code fragment needs to be added to the .pubxml file to simplify these paths. The entire profile can be found in the PackagePath.pubxml file in the PackageSample project.

```xml
<PropertyGroup>
  <PackagePath Condition=" '$(PackagePath)'=='' ">website</PackagePath>
  <PackageDependsOn>
    $(PackageDependsOn);
    AddReplaceRuleForAppPath;
  </PackageDependsOn>
</PropertyGroup>

<Target Name="AddReplaceRuleForAppPath">
  <PropertyGroup>
    <_PkgPathFull Condition=" '$(WPPAllFilesInSingleFolder)'!='' ">
$([System.IO.Path]::GetFullPath($(WPPAllFilesInSingleFolder)))</_PkgPathFull>
    <!-- $(WPPAllFilesInSingleFolder) is not available on VS2010 so fall back to
$(_PackageTempDir) -->
    <_PkgPathFull Condition=" '$(_PkgPathFull)' == '' ">
$([System.IO.Path]::GetFullPath($(_PackageTempDir)))</_PkgPathFull>
  </PropertyGroup>

  <!-- escape the text into a regex -->
  <EscapeTextForRegularExpressions Text="$(_PkgPathFull)">
    <Output TaskParameter="Result" PropertyName="_PkgPathRegex" />
  </EscapeTextForRegularExpressions>

  <!-- add the replace rule to update the path -->
  <ItemGroup>
    <MsDeployReplaceRules Include="replaceFullPath">
      <Match>$(_PkgPathRegex)</Match>
      <Replace>$(PackagePath)</Replace>
    </MsDeployReplaceRules>
  </ItemGroup>
</Target>
```

In this fragment, you can see the *AddReplaceRuleForAppPath* target. This target is injected into the package process by appending it to the *PackageDependsOn* property. When this target is invoked, it will determine the full path to the temporary package folder. This path is converted to a regular-expression format by using the EscapeTextForRegularExpressions task. Then the value is appended to the MSDeployReplaceRules item list. As a result, when the package is created, the complex folder structure will be replaced with a folder named Website, defined in the *PackagePath* property. When you create the package after these changes, you can see the new structure of the created .zip file in Figure 3-19.

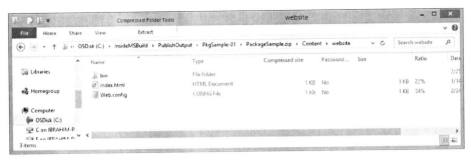

FIGURE 3-19 A simplified view of the package structure.

In Figure 3-19, you can see that the complex folder structure has been replaced with the Website folder, in which all the web content that will be published resides. Now that we've shown how to create better web packages, we will move on to the next sample.

How to publish a folder with Web Deploy

There are many scenarios in which it would be helpful to simply publish the contents of a local folder to a remote IIS server. For example, your web project may serve some binary content created by another group, and that content is not in source control. In this case, you can directly use Msdeploy. exe to publish that content. We will show how to publish a folder to a remote site using Web Deploy. The exact command that is required may vary based on how the IIS host is running Web Deploy. For this sample, we will be demonstrating this while publishing to Windows Azure Web Sites. Windows Azure Web Sites host MSDeploy using the Web Management Service (WMSvc), which is the common method for most third-party IIS hosting companies. Let's see how to accomplish this.

The Web Deploy provider that has the information on how to publish a folder is the contentPath provider, and this is what we will be using. When invoking MSDeploy to sync a folder, the basic command structure is as follows:

```
msdeploy.exe
    -verb:sync
    -source:contentPath="<source-path>"
    -dest:contentPath="<dest-path>"
```

Because we are attempting to synchronize two folders, the *sync* verb is used and we use *contentPath* for both the source and destination. The source folder that we want to publish is C:\InsideMSBuild\Ch03\FolderPublish\ToPublish, and we would like to publish it to the Media folder under the FolderPub site. Let's make a first attempt to figure out what the final command might look like:

```
msdeploy.exe
    -verb:sync
    -source:contentPath="C:\InsideMSBuild\ch03\FolderPublish\ToPublish"
    -dest:contentPath="FolderPub/Media"
```

This command would work great if the site you want to publish to was running on the local box. Because it is not, we will need to start adding some information to the destination to indicate the server against which this command should execute. We will need to add the following parameters to the command:

- **ComputerName** The URL, or computer name, that will handle the publish operation.

- **Username** The user name for the publish operation.

- **Password** The password for the publish operation.

- **AuthType** Describes what authentication mechanism is used. The options here are either Basic or NTLM. Typically, you will use Basic when Web Deploy is running under WMSvc and NTLM for when it is hosted using the Remote Agent Service.

In this case, the values that we will use for these are

- **ComputerName** *https://waws-prod-bay-001.publish.azurewebsites.windows.net/msdeploy .axd?site=FolderPub*

- **Username** *$FolderPub*

- **Password** *<Publishing password>*, where *Publishing password* is whatever password you have chosen

- **AuthType** Basic

For Windows Azure Web Sites, you can find these values in the publish profile, which you can download from the Azure portal. Let's add these values to the command:

```
msdeploy.exe
    -verb:sync -source:contentPath="C:\InsideMSBuild\ch03\FolderPublish\ToPublish"
    -dest:contentPath='FolderPub/Media'
        ,ComputerName="https://waws-prod-bay-001.publish.azurewebsites.windows.net/msdeploy.axd?
            site=FolderPub"
        ,UserName='$FolderPub'
        ,Password='%password%'
        ,AuthType='Basic'
    -enableRule:DoNotDeleteRule
    -whatif
```

In this command, we've added the destination values, as well as two additional options: *-enableRule:DoNotDeleteRule* and *-whatif*. We pass the *DoNotDeleteRule* to ensure that any files in the folder that are on the server but not the client remain on the server. For now, we are also passing *-whatif*, which displays the command's operations without actually performing them, but we will remove that when we are ready to publish the folder. You can find the result of this command in Figure 3-20.

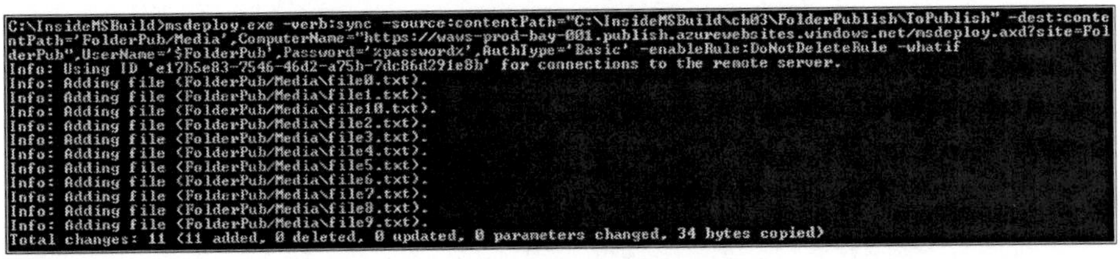

FIGURE 3-20 The result of invoking the Msdeploy.exe command.

At this point, we are ready to execute this command and publish the folder. You can find this command in the samples for Chapter 3 in the file FolderPublish\publishFolder-standard.cmd. There is another cmd file in that same folder, called PublishFolder-auto.cmd. This file shows how you can use this same technique with the -dest:auto provider. We won't cover that here, but it is in the samples for you to reference.

In this chapter, we have covered a lot of new material, including the Publish Web dialog box, updates to website project publishing, packaging, publish profiles, and more. That's a lot of material to discuss in just a few pages, and we didn't even cover all the new features. This chapter should serve as a solid starting point for your journey in web publishing. From here, the best thing to do is practice. If you get stuck, try StackOverflow.com (and you can typically find Sayed hanging around there as well—if you see him, say hello).

What do you think of this book?

We want to hear from you!
To participate in a brief online survey, please visit:

microsoft.com/learning/booksurvey

Tell us how well this book meets your needs—what works effectively, and what we can do better. Your feedback will help us continually improve our books and learning resources for you.

Thank you in advance for your input!

Index

Symbols and Numbers

$(MSBuildExtensionsPath)$ property, 21
.*publishSettings* file, 66, 68, 72
.*pubxml* file
    comparison to .*publishSettings* file, 66
    for building web packages, 71–73
    profile specific transforms, 80–83
    replace rules in, 87–88
.*sln* (solution file), 1–3, 20–22
.*targets* file, 13–14, 17
.wpp targets, 74–75

A

accessing
    diagnostic logs, 42
    operational logs, 43
account authentication, 52
activities. *See* workflow activities
Add Config Transform command, 80–81
Add Transform menu option, 14, 17
adding
    build agents to build controllers, 48–50
    classes to Visual Studio packages, 57–60
    comments to workflow activities, 47
    content to Visual Studio packages, 60
    NuGet packages, 9
    sections to build page, 55
AddReplaceRuleForAppPath target, 87
AfterCopyFiles target, 23–25
AfterTargets attribute, 21
All Build Definitions feature, 33–34
analytic logs, 44
AnalyzeCode targets, 21–22

B

annotations, 47
App.config transforms, 9, 14–16
App.Debug.config transform, 15–16
App.Release.config transform, 15–16
applications
    debugging, 15–16
    developing, 9–14
    updating, 14–19
Architecture attribute, 4–6
authentication, account, 52
Auto-Surround With Sequence, 46–47
Azure SDK 1.8, 65

batching, 39–41
BeforeTargets attribute, 21
build agents, 48–50
build configurations
    application, 14–16
    project, 69
build controllers
    adding build agent to existing, 48–50
    diagnostic logs for, 41–43
    on-premise, 51–54
    operational and analytic logs for, 43–44
    single, 31–32
build definitions
    all build definitions feature, 33–34
    drop locations for, 31
    filtering, 33–34
    hosted build definition selection for, 31
    marking favorite, 34
    pausing, 38
    storing favorite, 34
    web access to team, 35

About the authors

 SAYED IBRAHIM HASHIMI has a computer engineering degree from the University of Florida. He works at Microsoft as a program manager, creating better web development tools. Previously, he was a Microsoft Visual C# MVP. This is Sayed's fourth book on MSBuild. Sayed also has written for several publications, including *MSDN Magazine*. Sayed has also spoken at various tech conferences, including TechED. Before joining Microsoft, Sayed worked as a developer and independent consultant for companies ranging from Fortune 500 corporations to start-ups.

 WILLIAM BARTHOLOMEW is a lead software development engineer at Microsoft Corporation in Redmond, Washington. He is a member of the Developer Division Engineering Systems group, which includes the build lab responsible for building and shipping Microsoft Visual Studio.

CPSIA information can be obtained at www.ICGtesting.com
Printed in the USA
BVOW022118160413

318240BV00002BA/4/P